the vastu home

JULIET PEGRUM

DUNCAN BAIRD PUBLISHERS

LONDON

the vastu home

Juliet Pegrum

First published in the United Kingdom and Ireland in 2002 by
Duncan Baird Publishers Ltd
Sixth Floor
Castle House
75–76 Wells Street
London W1T 3QH

Conceived, created and designed by Duncan Baird Publishers

Managing Editor: Judy Barratt
Editor: Lucy Latchmore
Managing Designer: Manisha Patel
Picture Research: Cecilia Weston-Baker
Decorative Artwork: Jenny Bakker

British Library Cataloguing-in-Publication Data:
A CIP record for this book is available from the British Library.

ISBN: 1-904292-19-4

10 9 8 7 6 5 4 3 2 1

Typeset in Agfa Rotis and Univers
Colour reproduction by Scanhouse, Malaysia
Printed in Singapore by Imago

I would like to dedicate this book to all the kind teachers who have guided me on a pilgrimage of discovery – especially to Dr Babu who first initiated me into the practice of Vastu. I hope that this book will similarly inspire all readers who wish to live in harmony with their environment.

contents

Introduction

Have you ever experienced inexplicable feelings of happiness and peace when visiting certain places? Perhaps on a mountain top, admiring the beauty of the view, you felt a profound sense of connectedness with nature; or, when visiting a temple or church, awed by the magnificence of the construction, you experienced feelings of upliftment and joy.

I have spent lengthy periods in India over the past ten years, pursuing my deep interest in yoga. When visiting certain temples and sacred sites, I often wondered at the waves of serenity and joy that washed over me as I entered these spaces. As an interior designer I was fascinated by their emotional and spiritual power. What, I asked myself, was the source of this dynamic relationship between the environment, the emotions of the mind, and the sensations of the body?

It was the discovery of Vastu that provided the answers to my questions. I first came across the word Vastu while working as an interior designer in Jaipur, India. The company employing me was building a new workshop, but had encountered many obstacles to the completion of the project. My Indian colleagues were convinced that they could have avoided these delays by consulting a Vastu expert at the start of the work. Upon enquiry I discovered that Vastu is an ancient Indian science of architecture and design, which aims to align living spaces with unseen spiritual and natural laws.

The connection between the spiritual and physical dimensions of human experience immediately caught my attention. My quest to learn more led me to Dr Babu, a Vastu practitioner who agreed to teach me his art.

In learning about Vastu I discovered the basis for the emotional and spiritual connection between humans and the environment that I had already experienced so profoundly. Gradually, I came to understand the implications of Vastu for the modern world – how we can use this wisdom in practical ways to improve our living spaces, and consequently the quality of our lives.

In this book I present a distillation of my insights in the hope that they will inspire you to reflect more consciously on your environment. Ask yourself: are you happy and at peace in your living spaces? Do they fulfil your deepest needs and desires? Are you inspired by their beauty?

If you answered negatively to any of these questions, this book should bring you many benefits. By introducing the spirit of Vastu into your home, you will be taking positive steps toward the creation of living spaces blessed with positive energies that uplift the spirits and energize both body and mind, a home whose outer beauty is a true reflection of its inner harmony.

How to use this book

This book seeks to translate the wisdom of Vastu into terms that are relevant to our modern Western homes. It is intended as an inspirational guide, offering simple and practical ways to apply Vastu to the home.

To reinterpret this ancient science for the modern world, its complex roots must be understood. To this end the first chapter of the book explains the historical and mythological background of Vastu, placing it in context with the other Vedic sciences of yoga and Ayurveda. This is followed by an explanation of the theoretical basis for Vastu, together with a description of the tools used to implement its theories within the home.

The second chapter approaches Vastu on a more dynamic and personal level. In addition to offering advice on choosing a new home, this section outlines ways to create the appropriate atmosphere and mood within your current environment. According to Vastu only when we attune our interiors to our individual needs and the specific functions of each room can we create environments in which we feel totally comfortable and at peace.

Having grasped the basic principles of Vastu in the first two chapters, we then apply this knowledge to specific rooms in both the home and workplace. At the beginning of each room section a small box (divided into nine squares) placed next to the title is an immediate indicator of the ideal location according to the cardinal and intercardinal directions (North is always at the top). The comprehensive approach includes specific details of layout and design and ensures that there is something for everyone – whether you are redesigning your home, or seeking simple ways to bring Vastu into your existing interiors.

The fourth chapter extends the practice of Vastu to our outdoor garden spaces, as we follow the principles established earlier in the book to create gardens that harmonize with the home as a whole.

You will find a number of floor plans for individual rooms in the third chapter, and a garden plan in the fourth chapter. These layouts provide visual correlatives for the information supplied in the text. They represent practicable ideals, demonstrating how Vastu principles can work in reality.

However, these plans are in no sense prescriptive. Rather, they are intended to serve as gentle guides, illustrating possible arrangements of furniture or features. In practice the precise proportions of your rooms and garden, the positions of existing features, and the items of furniture that you already possess will dictate the choice of layouts available to you. In recognition of these constraints, various remedies have been suggested to help you overcome any major problems that you may encounter.

When designing your home the most important thing to remember is that it is you who will be living there. Vastu seeks to harmonize the home with the minds and bodies of the occupants as well as the cosmos. It is therefore essential that whatever advice is given in the text, the interiors you create are adapted to suit you. Only then will you achieve the central goal of Vastu – to feel truly at one with your environment.

understanding vastu

VASTU IS AN ANCIENT SCIENCE OF PLACEMENT AND DESIGN THAT WAS DEVELOPED IN INDIA MORE THAN 3,000 YEARS AGO. IT IS A PRACTICE THAT AIMS TO CREATE THE PERFECT LIVING ENVIRONMENT BY ALIGNING BOTH THE HOME AND GARDEN WITH THE COSMOS. IN THIS CHAPTER WE TAKE A JOURNEY THROUGH THE HISTORY OF VASTU TO DISCOVER ITS FOUNDATION IN HINDU MYTH AND TO UNDERSTAND ITS BASIC PRINCIPLES. WE ARE INTRODUCED TO THE MOST IMPORTANT TOOL OF THE VASTU PRACTITIONER – THE VASTU PURUSHA MANDALA, WHICH MAPS THE COMPLEX FORCES OF THE UNIVERSE AND PROVIDES AN ARCHITECTURAL BLUEPRINT FOR THE HOME. WE ALSO DISCUSS EACH OF THE FORCES ENCAPSULATED IN THE MANDALA: THE CARDINAL DIRECTIONS, THE FIVE ELEMENTS, THE THREE *GUNAS* AND, ULTIMATELY, *PRANA* – THE ENERGY OF LIFE ITSELF.

What is Vastu Vidya?

Vastu Vidya (often shortened to Vastu) translates literally as the "wisdom of dwelling places". An ancient spiritual science of architecture, Vastu belongs to the geomantic tradition of the Indian subcontinent and is a distant cousin (some believe ancestor) of the more widely recognized Chinese practice of Feng Shui. It is a system that provides a set of principles for the construction, layout and interior design of houses, temples and even whole cities.

Vastu is closely linked to other ancient Indian practices, such as Ayurveda – the principal traditional medical system of India – and yoga, a path to spiritual progress via a disciplining of the mind and body. Both Ayurveda and yoga enable practitioners to harmonize their physical and mental being with the natural balance of the cosmos. Vastu works to protect this harmony between body, mind and universe by creating living spaces that are similarly attuned with the cosmic balance and are oriented according to the movement of the sun, the electromagnetic field of the Earth, the five elements (see pp.28–31) and the three *gunas* (see pp.32–3). When alignment is achieved, the living space echoes the basic structure of the universe, and *prana* (the energy believed to sustain all living things; see pp.34–7) flows freely through the space, bringing health, happiness, peace and wellbeing to its inhabitants.

The development of Vastu

Scholars believe that Vastu originated more than 3,000 years ago. The system was first alluded to in the *Yajurveda*. This is one of the four ancient sacred Hindu texts known collectively as *Vedas*, and is believed to date from before 1200BCE. Vedic philosophy describes the principles of Vastu as gifts from the gods to humankind. Semi-divine beings known as *rishis* are believed to have intuited the wisdom of Vastu during their spiritual and meditative practices. According to Hindu myth, this knowledge was originally provided by Brahma, the supreme creator of the universe, who passed the information, via Shiva, the god of destruction, to Vishwakarma, the primordial architect of the universe.

Vastu was originally a sacred, oral tradition that was taught only to priests and sincere spiritual aspirants. In recent years archeologists have discovered some of the earliest written treatises on the subject, dating back to the sixth century CE. Two of the most comprehensive of these manuscripts were composed during the tenth century CE. These are the *Manasara*, authored by Rishi Manasara, and the *Mayamata*, authored by the venerable teacher and architect Maya. These manuscripts were produced during the Chola period in South India – a time of great renaissance for classical ideas and ancient Vedic architecture.

Vastu today

Although originally interpreted for ancient Indian civilizations, the principles of Vastu can equally be applied to Western homes today – the energies of the cosmos are timeless and exert their influence around the entire globe. Vastu can therefore be applied to any style of home in any location, from the most elaborate palaces in southern India to modern loft-style apartments in New York.

In the West we tend to have rather superficial attitudes toward interior and garden design; Vastu offers us a more holistic approach. Treating the home as a complete unit, Vastu works to create a sense of connection and flow between rooms, a movement of energy throughout the overall structures of house and garden. Within individual rooms Vastu strives to achieve harmony between function and design, to develop a definable character or mood in keeping with the purpose of each space. Such harmony encourages us to feel centred and at ease, fully engaged with the unique energies of individual rooms.

Vastu lends itself to a wide variety of interiors, but in all cases it stresses the importance of creating light and space within the home. (As we will see, a few carefully chosen objects or furnishings can serve to promote positive energy; too many will impede its flow.) In addition Vastu focuses on the placement of furniture and the strategic use of colour, shape, texture and natural elements – tools we can use in any home to energize each room.

right *The Brihadeshwara temple in Tanjore, Tamil Nadu – a magnificent example of classical Vedic architecture from the Chola period.* inset *Brahma, the Hindu god of creation, passes a page of the* Vedas *to a devotee. His four faces symbolize the four* Vedas *and his four hands denote each of the cardinal directions.*

The myth of Vastu Purusha

For thousands of years human civilizations have used myths as a means to describe and assimilate the mysteries of the universe. Hindu mythology is particularly colourful and rich, containing a large pantheon of gods, demi-gods and demons that represent different aspects or elements of the natural world. Together these divine beings provide a vocabulary that allows us to communicate about – and at some level understand – the transcendent and invisible forces of the universe.

The science of Vastu uses the mythical figure of Vastu Purusha to convey its basic principles. Purusha is a cosmic spirit whose body acts as a symbol for the forces believed to govern the cosmos and the human body – the same forces with which Vastu seeks to align the home.

There are numerous variations of the myth that tells of Purusha's origins. One describes an omnipotent entity without name or form, who existed at the dawn of time, blocking the sky and Earth in all directions and threatening to consume the world. In desperation the gods asked Brahma (the supreme creator) what they should do to overcome this demon. Brahma instructed the deities to press the entity to the ground by sitting on its various parts. Taking his seat above the navel, Brahma blessed the demon, making him immortal.

A detail from the Brihadeshwara temple showing Shiva, the god of destruction. Ganesh, the remover of obstacles, is carved above the alcove – in Vastu he is used to deflect negative energies away from the home.

He gave him the form of a man, with his stomach facing the Earth, and declared that he was the guardian of earthly creation and architecture. This form became known as Vastu Purusha.

Blessed with divine power, Purusha bestows health, wealth and happiness on those who design their homes with reverence for the natural world by adhering to the rules of Vastu. His portrayal as a demon reminds us that if we ignore the natural balance of the universe we invite disaster into our lives. Many Indians believe that Purusha inhabits every building, with his physical posture aligned along the northeast to southwest diagonal. (The head lies in the northeast and the feet and folded legs in the southwest.) This belief forms the basis for the practices of Vastu.

The Vastu Purusha Mandala

Mandalas are geometric representations of the cosmos. In Hindu and Buddhist traditions they are used as aids to meditation – by focusing the mind on the mandala, the meditator can learn to achieve a profound sense of oneness with the universe.

The Vastu Purusha Mandala is most unusual in that it is employed by Vastu practitioners as a tool for the orientation and design of living spaces, rather than as an aid to meditation. Their aim is to harmonize the living space, rather than themselves, with the natural balance of the cosmos. This core difference in function is reflected in the appearance of the Vastu Purusha Mandala, for while most mandalas are circular in shape (the Sanskrit word *mandala* means "circle"), the Vastu Purusha Mandala forms a square.

The symbol of the square

For centuries human civilizations have used symbols to make sense of the world around them. In India the symbol of the square is called the *sakala* and represents the Earth in its fixed aspect (as opposed to the circle, which symbolizes the movement of the Earth). The symmetry of the square perfectly contains the eight compass directions: the four sides represent the cardinal directions (north, south, east and west), while the four corners represent the inter-cardinal directions (northeast, southeast, southwest and northwest). If we use the mandala square as a blueprint for the layout of our homes, we can align them with the cosmos: the ground floor represents the earth; the walls, the four directions; and the roof, the heavens.

Within the square

Everything that is contained within the square represents the cosmic forces of the universe in their natural rhythm and order, while everything outside the square represents the chaos of the unknown.

As Purusha is the mythical embodiment of these cosmic forces, his body is represented within the mandala square. In accordance with the myth, he is depicted lying belly down over the earth with his body oriented along the northeast–southwest axis. The elements (see pp.28–31) correspond to different parts of his body: Ether lies at his head; Air, Water and Fire lie across his middle; and Earth lies at his feet.

(By association, the elements are therefore thought to govern the intercardinal quadrants of the mandala square.)

However, it is not only Purusha who resides within the square. According to myth 45 deities pinned him to the ground. These deities are represented on Vastu diagrams that show the division of the mandala square into 45 sections. Generally, however, only nine of the deities are thought to play a major role in Vastu Vidya. Eight of these are known collectively as the *Vasus* (meaning "that which surrounds"): they are Kubera in the north, Indra in the east, Yama in the south, Varuna in the west, Soma in the northeast,

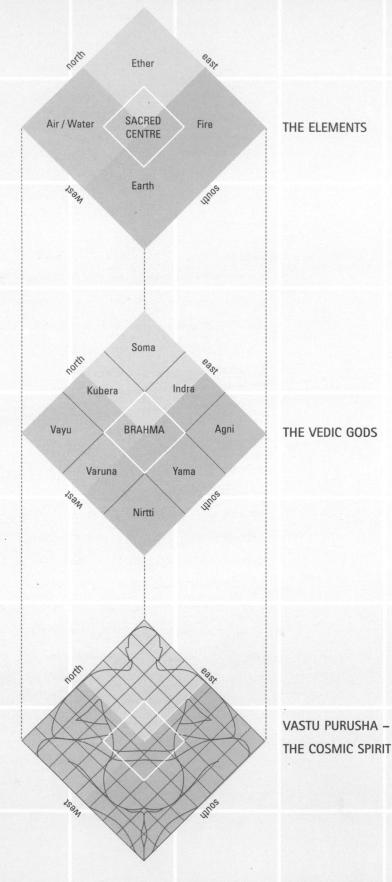

THE ELEMENTS

THE VEDIC GODS

VASTU PURUSHA – THE COSMIC SPIRIT

THE MANDALA: LAYERS OF MEANING

top The intercardinal quadrants of the mandala are associated with the five elements: Ether (northeast) invites sacred energy (*prana*) into the home; Fire (southeast) is linked with heat and light; Earth (southwest) is linked with tolerance and heaviness; Air and Water share the northwest – Air is linked with movement, Water with transition and cleansing.

middle Each cardinal and intercardinal space has a presiding Vedic god. The north is occupied by Kubera, god of wealth and ayurvedic medicine. Soma, the god of knowledge and spiritual wealth, resides in the northeast. The east is home to Indra, god of renewal. In the southeast is Agni, god of fire. Yama, in the south, is Lord of Death, who guards our souls. Nirtti, in the southwest, represents longevity. In the west lies Varuna, god of water. The northwest is home to Vayu, god of winds, who circulates the cosmic energy. Brahma, supreme creator deity, governs the sacred centre.

bottom The figure of Purusha is represented in the mandala square with his head in the northeast, his feet in the southwest, his left arm in the north and his right leg in the south. His belly covers the nine central squares, which make up the *Brahmasthana* – the sacred space.

Agni in the southeast, Nirtti in the south-west and Vayu in the northwest. The ninth, and most important, deity is Brahma, who occupies the sacred centre. Each deity exhibits unique characteristics and influences a different sphere of worldly life (see diagram, opposite).

Tuning into the mandala

Vastu's aim of achieving harmony with the cosmos stems from an understanding (shared by the ancient *rishis* and modern physicists alike) that all matter is composed of condensed energy vibrating at different frequencies. Although we tend to imagine that external objects are solid and separate from ourselves, in fact they constantly emit vibrations, which interact positively or negatively with both us and other objects.

This interconnectedness means that each one of our actions, however small, affects the balance of the cosmos. Vedic civilization demonstrated an awareness of this fact in its profound respect for creation, a belief in the divinity of all things. Even stones were considered to be alive – builders would use only middle-aged stones for construction, deeming both young and old unsuitable.

Accordingly, if we design our homes in line with Vastu principles, they become our personal mandalas, in tune with both our true selves and the world that surrounds us. Whenever we enter our homes, we become aware of our intrinsic place within the universe, a sense of connection with all things that brings happiness and fulfilment to our lives.

The sacred centre

"The wise must avoid tormenting his limbs with the limbs of the house, if not, sorrows innumerable will fall upon the limbs of the owner of the house."
MANASARA (c.900ce)

Fundamental to Vastu is the importance of the sacred centre; this is represented by the centre of the Vastu Purusha Mandala (see pp.20–23), which corresponds to the central area of any space.

When we apply the mandala to either the home as a whole, or an individual room, we imagine the physical form of Purusha lying face down in the room, oriented along the northeast–southwest axis. The centre of the mandala covers the heart and navel of Vastu Purusha's "body". These areas are believed to be his most sensitive, with a concentration of vulnerable or weak points called *Marma sthanas*. Accordingly, the principles of Vastu state that the most

vulnerable points of a room are located in the middle. You can protect this area by keeping it as clear and open as possible – free from heavy masonry and pieces of furniture, or from architectural features, such as pillars and beams.

Keeping the central area of a room uncluttered is also important because it is the *Brahmasthana* – the seat of Brahma, who is the god associated with the origin of the universe and a symbol of creation. If we keep this space clear, revering it as sacred, Brahma's spiritual power will then radiate outward into the rest of the room, bringing happiness, health and prosperity to each of the inhabitants.

The centre of this room has been kept clear of furniture to protect Vastu Purusha's vulnerable points. The placement of the rug over the centre reminds occupants that this area is the sacred seat of Brahma.

The cardinal directions

The cardinal directions, or compass points, provide spatial coordinates that enable us to align our homes and gardens with the electromagnetic field of the Earth. The subtle vibrations of this field also constitute one of the key forces or energies that affect our living spaces.

Ancient *rishis* imagined the Earth's magnetic field to be a complex grid of energy lines running from north to south and east to west. They viewed the Earth as a giant magnet with the north at the positive pole and the south at the negative pole. Western science supports these ideas with a body of evidence suggesting that our atmosphere is charged with electro-magnetic energy produced by negatively and positively charged ions.

Scientists believe that the Earth's intrinsic magnetic properties have existed for at least 3,000 million years. What produces this electromagnetic field remains a mystery, but it was clear to the ancient *rishis* that these energies profoundly affect the human body. (The body produces its own electromagnetic field, which interacts with that of the Earth.)

In terms of human consciousness, the cardinal directions are highly significant because they define not only our spatial

Yoga and meditation are traditionally practised in the morning, facing the east – the rays of the rising sun are believed to encourage inner illumination. Suffused with morning sunlight, this alcove at the Devigargh Palace in India provides the perfect place for such activities.

but also our metaphysical place in the world. Together their opposing forces represent the contradictions that lie within us, as well as the dualities of the external world, such as hot and cold, light and dark.

Furthermore, each direction possesses individual significance. The east is the direction from which the sun rises, ushering in each new day with its promise of new beginnings, optimism and hope. Its antithesis, the west – the direction of the setting sun – reminds us of endings and the darkness of the unknown, but also promotes reflection and peace after a long day's toil. The north indicates the region of divine immortality, while the south symbolizes the past, the realm of our ancestors. At the centre is the zenith, the heart of all earthly activities.

The home of the five elements

According to the ancient Vedic scriptures, the entire physical universe is made up of five basic elements, known as the *Maha Bhutas* or Great Elements – Earth, Water, Fire, Air and Ether. To create harmony between a home, its inhabitants and the universe, the balance of elements within the home must reflect those of both the human body and the cosmos. Vastu provides the tools to achieve this balance using the elements themselves and their symbolic representations.

When analyzing the distribution of elements within a space, we must divide it along the north–south and east–west axes to form four quadrants. According to Vastu Earth resides in the southwest quadrant, Fire in the southeast, Air and Water in the northwest and Ether in the northeast.

Essentially, each element is condensed energy vibrating at a specific frequency. The lower the frequency, the more solid the element's structure. At the bottom of the spectrum, with the lowest frequency, is Earth. This is followed consecutively by Water, Fire, Air and finally Ether (the subtlest element, equivalent to space).

The unique properties of each element mean that the different quadrants are suited to particular activities. For example, the inertness of Earth in the southwest makes this part of a building perfect for sleeping; the restless nature of Air and Water in the northwest quadrant provides the ideal conditions for transitory activities, such as bathing. The Fire element makes the southeast quadrant an obvious choice for cooking, and the focus provided by Ether renders the northeast ideal for study or meditation.

When all of these elements are correctly balanced, with the functions of the home distributed accordingly, the space is said to be in perfect harmony. However, in most homes the layout of rooms does not accord with the Vastu ideal. This can result in a conflict between the actual function of the room and the element naturally resident in that location. Where this occurs we need to appease the resident element, while also strengthening the element appropriate to the room's function, in order to achieve harmony.

One way to strengthen or appease an element is to represent it symbolically in the appropriate quadrant of the space. For example, if Fire is lacking in the southeast of your living room, having a fireplace or some lighted candles in this region will strengthen the element's presence. Similarly, a plant or stone statue set in the southwest will strengthen Earth; a water feature or a simple bowl of water in the northwest will encourage Water; the gentle breeze from an open window in the northwest will promote Air; clearing some space in the northeast will stimulate Ether.

However, there are other ways by which particular elements can be encouraged in the home. Each element is associated with a specific shape and bodily sense. Earth is symbolized by a square, which means that a square piece of furniture, such as a table, will strengthen Earth in a room. Similarly, circular or fluid shapes encourage Water; crescent shapes encourage Air; triangular shapes encourage Fire; and diamond shapes encourage Ether.

Each of the five bodily senses is attuned to a particular element, so by appealing to certain senses within a space, we can strengthen the corresponding elements. The pleasing scents of flowers and incense promote Earth by stimulating our sense of smell. A display of fruit and vegetables – perhaps a bowl of waxy lemons or some brightly coloured peppers – encourage Water by stimulating taste. Visually striking objects, such as beautiful paintings or unusual sculptures, appeal to sight and strengthen Fire, while richly textured fabrics, such as heavy brocades and soft wools, appeal to touch and stimulate Air. Likewise, soothing music or the tinkle of wind chimes stimulate hearing and encourage Ether.

above left *In the northwest quadrant of this room, a mirror and a water feature strengthen Water, and the texture of cotton cushions encourages Air.* above right *In the northeast an abundance of light and a lack of clutter promote Ether.* below left *In the southwest square furniture and a selection of plants strengthen Earth.* below right *In the southeast a bold painting and the striking orange wall-colour stimulate Fire.*

 The *gunas*

According to Vedic scriptures, the five elements are composed of three types or qualities of energy: *sattva*, *tamas* and *rajas*. They are known as the *gunas* – the word *guna* means "part of a whole". *Sattva* represents the positive energy of clarity, cohesion and understanding. *Tamas* is the opposing energy to *sattva* and represents inertia and heaviness, dissolution and destruction. *Rajas* is the energy that moves from *sattva* to *tamas*, manifesting itself as restlessness and activity.

The three *gunas* exist in each of the elements in varying proportions, providing them with their characteristic qualities. The inert energy of *tamas* predominates in the solid Earth element; the clarity of *sattva* predominates in Ether; and the restless energy of *rajas* predominates in Fire, Air and Water.

The distribution of the *gunas* within a building or room reflects this relationship with the elements. The northeast quadrant of a space is the home of Ether and *sattva*. *Tamas* presides in the opposite quadrant in the southwest Earth corner. *Rajas* dominates in the southeast Fire quadrant and in the northwest Air and Water quadrant.

Balancing the *gunas* within a space can help to balance the elements, and vice versa. In Vastu each *guna* is linked with a different shade and tone of colour, so the

This colour scheme of rajasic oranges combined with the tamasic qualities of indigo and dark brown is particularly appropriate for rooms located in the south or west where both rajas *and* tamas *predominate.*

balance of the *gunas* within a room or home can be manipulated by introducing specific shades and tones of colour. Cooler, lighter colours, such as pale blues and greens, encourage *sattva*. These hues are ideal for rooms with a northeast location, or for rooms, such as a study or library, that benefit from an atmosphere of clarity and understanding. Strong and fiery colours, such as reds, oranges and pinks, are rajasic and will stimulate excitement and activity – they are particularly appropriate for northwest or southeast locations. Dark colours, such as indigo, mahogany and ebony, absorb light and are tamasic in nature. They are most suitable for south-west rooms, but can be used sparingly in any space as accent colours to give a sense of rootedness and depth.

Prana – cosmic energy

According to the Vedic texts, where there is life, there is *prana*. The word *prana* means the breath of Purusha or the breath of life in general. Equivalent to the Chinese concept of *chi, prana* is the fundamental life-force or energy that animates all things. It is an extremely subtle energy, which Hindus believe can only be experienced directly during states of deep meditation.

The three Vedic disciplines of yoga, Ayurveda and Vastu are all based upon this understanding of *prana*. Together they form a holistic system of wellbeing that ensures that the patterns of *prana* within our bodies and surroundings reflect the flow of *prana* through the cosmos.

Both yoga and Ayurveda seek to maintain an optimum flow of *prana* through the body. Yoga emphasizes breathing and Ayurveda concentrates on eating habits as being the primary factors influencing the body's energy patterns. Vastu works alongside these disciplines, so that the energy profiles of the body and the home mirror one another.

Through their meditation practices the ancient *rishis* came to understand the path of *prana* through a space and how best to encourage it. They noted that *prana* meandered from the northeast (home of Ether and *sattva*) toward the southwest (home of Earth and *tamas*), avoiding the

A series of open windows and doors allows the energizing rays of natural sunlight to permeate these interior spaces, promoting the flow of prana *throughout.*

sacred central area of a room (see pp.24–5). On the basis of this pattern, the *rishis* advised keeping the northeast area of any room open, while blocking the southwest of the room with heavy furniture to prevent *prana* escaping.

There are three main ways of ensuring that *prana* moves freely through the home. The first, and simplest, is to see that our rooms are free from excess clutter, which can impede the pranic flow. The second is to achieve the correct balance of the elements and *gunas* (see pp.28–31 and 32–3); and the third is to maximize the amount of light flowing throughout the home.

Natural sunlight, which combines all the colours of the rainbow, is the most balanced and energizing source of light. The importance of sunlight is reflected in its universal significance as a symbol of the divine. According to Hindu mythology, the sun is the earthly manifestation of the Lord of the east – the sun god Surya (a Sanskrit word meaning "to shine"). In India the energy or sunlight produced by the sun is therefore known as the "breath of God".

The ancient *rishis* recommended that we should design and orient our homes to maximize our exposure to natural sunlight. They believed that it is better to have the potential for too much sunlight than too little (the idea being that incoming light can, if necessary, be muted by translucent curtains or blinds without impeding the pranic flow). Not only did they recommend homes with an abundance of windows and doors, they also suggested that the different types of rooms or areas within our

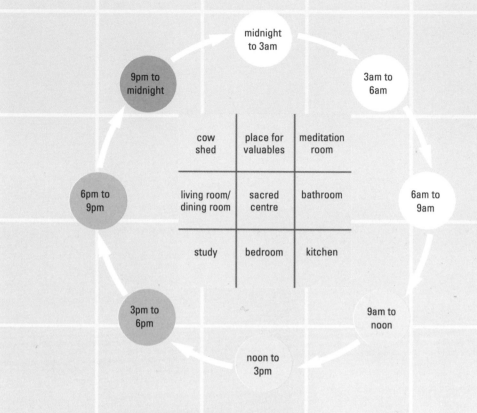

HARNESSING THE SUN

The Vastu ideal is to designate the different rooms or areas of our homes so as to optimize our exposure to natural light (and so *prana*). This diagram shows the position of the sun in relation to the layout of a typical Indian home. Meditation is traditionally practised in the early hours, before sunrise. Once occupants are bathed and dressed, they spend the morning preparing food for the whole day. The hottest part of the day is a time of rest, and the cooler afternoons and evenings are spent in study and relaxation, before milking the cows at the end of the day.

homes should be determined according to the direction of sunlight at particular times of day (see diagram, opposite). This helps to maintain the natural, diurnal rhythms of our bodies and minds, which fluctuate according to the movement of the Earth around the sun.

Morning sunlight, which comes from the northeast, is especially beneficial in the home because it contains a large proportion of ultraviolet light. This functions as a purifier, killing off disease-carrying bacteria, as well as providing a reliable source of vitamin D. Furthermore, it helps to stimulate *prana*, which flows naturally from the northeast (see p.34) of the home.

Built in 1728 this astronomical instrument from the Jantar Mantar observatory in Jaipur, northern India, tells the time and ascertains the position of heavenly bodies in the northern and southern hemispheres.

living vastu

VASTU IS CONCERNED WITH THE LAND THAT SURROUNDS A DWELLING AS WELL AS WITH THE NATURE OF THE BUILDING ITSELF. USEFUL FOR BOTH PROSPECTIVE BUYERS AND CURRENT OWNERS, THIS CHAPTER OUTLINES SOME BASIC TOPOGRAPHICAL AND ARCHITECTURAL PRINCIPLES OF VASTU, GIVING PRACTICAL ADVICE ON HOW THESE CAN BE APPLIED TO WESTERN BUILDINGS. MOVING INSIDE THE HOME WE DISCOVER THE IMPORTANCE OF CREATING THE RIGHT MOOD OR ATMOSPHERE – OF PERSONALIZING OUR SURROUNDINGS TO SUIT OUR INDIVIDUAL NEEDS AND DESIRES. THIS CAN BE ACHIEVED THROUGH THE USE OF COLOUR AND DESIGN AS WELL AS THROUGH THE INTRODUCTION OF IMAGES, OBJECTS AND ARTEFACTS. WE ALSO LOOK AT DIFFERENT TYPES OF STORAGE AS WE EXPLORE PRACTICAL STRATEGIES FOR DECLUTTERING THE INTERIORS OF THE HOME.

Orienting the home

Before we can apply the Vastu Purusha Mandala to our home, we need to orient the house according to the cardinal and intercardinal directions. To do this we can either use a compass or, more simply, observe the position of the sun on the horizon in the morning and evening to locate east and west respectively.

Marking each of the cardinal directions, draw plans of your "plot" (your garden and the land on which your home is situated); each level of your home – incorporating any cellars, terraces or balconies; and each individual room. Try to capture the proportions as accurately as you can. Make sure that you include on the plans all doors and windows, and any architectural features, such as pillars, fireplaces, alcoves and balconies.

Draw a square around each plan to represent the mandala (the size of the square is determined by the longest edge of the plan). Divide each square into quarters along the north–south and east–west axes. From this you can establish the basic distribution of the five elements and the three *gunas*, as well as the path of *prana* from the northeast, around the northwest and southeast edges, toward the southwest.

Ideally, this energy profile should inform the layout of each space. The chart opposite summarizes the best distribution of rooms within the home, and subsequent chapters detail preferred layouts for specific rooms and outdoor spaces. Experiment with different arrangements of furniture to discover which layouts suit the specifications of your home and fulfil your needs.

ROOM	IDEAL LOCATION(S)	ELEMENT(S)	*GUNA(S)*	HOURS OF ENERGY
Living room	northwest or west	Air / Water or Earth and Air / Water	*rajas* or *tamas* and *rajas*	9pm – midnight or 6pm – 9pm
Kitchen	southeast	Fire	*rajas*	9am – noon
Dining room	west	Earth and Air / Water	*tamas* and *rajas*	6pm – 9pm
Study	north or southwest	Air / Water and Ether or Earth	*rajas* and *sattva* or *tamas*	midnight – 3am or 3pm – 6pm
Bathroom	east or southwest or northwest	Ether and Fire or Earth or Air / Water	*sattva* and *rajas* or *tamas* or *rajas*	6am – 9am or 3pm – 6pm or 9pm – midnight
Master bedroom	south or southwest	Fire and Earth or Earth	*rajas* and *tamas* or *tamas*	noon – 3pm or 3pm – 6pm
Young child's room	east	Ether and Fire	*sattva* and *rajas*	6am – 9am
Teenager's room	north	Air / Water and Ether	*rajas* and *sattva*	midnight – 3am
Guest room	northwest	Air / Water	*rajas*	9pm – midnight
"Zone of tranquillity"	northeast	Ether	*sattva*	3am – 6am

THE IDEAL ENERGY PROFILE FOR THE HOME

This chart shows the ideal positions for each room within your home according to the elements, *gunas* and hours of energy (determined by the position of the sun) that characterize each location. When analyzing your home use this information to pinpoint well- and poorly positioned rooms. You can also use the table to find out which elements, *gunas* and kinds of light you need to encourage in order to redress any energy imbalances.

Choosing a Vastu home: the site

Vastu addresses every aspect of a potential living space, beginning with the shape of the site and the surrounding landscape. If you are choosing a new home, bear in mind some of the following basic principles.

The shape of the site

According to Vastu, the square is the perfect shape in which to dwell because it reflects the Vedic concept of the universe – it represents all four cardinal directions and provides a balance of the five elements and three *gunas*. It is also a strong, stable shape that offers protection from external forces. An alternative is the rectangle – a shape with characteristics similar to the square.

Ideally, then, you are looking for sites that are either square or rectangular. If you have a choice between these shapes, bear in mind the different energies that each induces. While a square possesses an energy suited to active pursuits, such as sports, rectangles have an energy that encourages more reflective pastimes, such as reading or creative endeavours.

Of course, you can always subdivide a site with fencing or hedging to create the shape (and corresponding energy) that you prefer. Such divisions also provide a useful remedy for the adverse effects caused by triangular, circular or irregularly shaped sites, which you should avoid if possible.

Clear space in the foreground, and the depression in the ground created by the pond, both attract prana *into the garden, while the trees in the background provide a block that contains the energy within the site.*

Because of their connection with the Fire element, triangular sites can have destructive effects on their inhabitants by creating an atmosphere of tension and anger. Less serious, but considered to be disruptive, are the effects of circular or otherwise rounded sites. These shapes are associated with Water and are believed to induce restlessness. While this may be appropriate for public spaces, such as auditoriums or sports stadiums where people come and go, it is not suitable for permanent dwellings.

The contours of the landscape

In general, Vastu recommends choosing relatively flat landscapes for human dwellings: a home perched on a hill will be exposed to the full rigours of the weather; a house built at the bottom of a valley will have limited access to sunlight. Of course, in some areas, hills cannot be avoided and you may need to manipulate the surroundings to create the Vastu ideal. Growing a shield of trees will provide protection from prevailing winds for hilltop homes; thinning dense vegetation around houses in valleys will help to maximize the flow of light and energy into them.

The contours of the site

According to the principles of Vastu, the ideal site for a home slopes gently upward to the southwest, with a depression to the northeast of the property. Such contours ensure that energy is unable to escape via the southwest and instead collects in the northeast. Few sites match this profile exactly, but you can achieve a similar effect

by planting trees or erecting a building to the southwest of the home and creating space in the northeast.

Energy obstructions

When choosing a site for a home, we need to be particularly aware of *vedhas* (external obstacles), such as graveyards, electricity pylons and industrial sites, which can disrupt the energies of a living space. To counteract the negative effects of any external obstacles, Hindus traditionally position deities and yantras (pictorial diagrams of the cosmos) around the home, facing toward the *vedha*, to deflect the *vedha*'s negative energy away from the site. For a similar result, try placing either a mirror, or any object that is sacred to you (whether secular or religious), in the area of your home that is closest to the source of the negative energy.

City dwelling

In the cramped conditions of the city, few homes are situated on self-contained sites – many people live in apartment buildings. Nevertheless, when choosing an apartment it is still important to consider the surroundings. Search for an apartment block with space around it – this will ensure good ventilation and an unobstructed flow of light and *prana* into each apartment. Try to avoid, too, apartment blocks that are overshadowed by larger, adjacent buildings.

As well as lack of space, noise pollution causes problems in the city. Look for homes on quieter back streets or, better still, in the suburbs.

◈ Choosing a Vastu home: the structure

"From his [Purusha's] navel was the atmosphere, from his head the sky was turned, from his feet the earth, from his ear the directions, thus they constructed worlds."
RIG VEDA (c.1200BCE)

The ancient manuscripts of Vastu outline a variety of architectural principles ranging from general rules of proportion and shape to more detailed specifications for individual features. When buying a home it is helpful to bear these guidelines in mind. Although originally intended for Indian houses, with some adjustment they can also be applied to Western living spaces.

The type of home

The ideal Vastu home is detached and therefore surrounded by space, but, as we have seen, increasing pressures on space in the Western world have resulted in many of us living in "attached" houses or apartments. When choosing an apartment consider its structure and position, as well as the surrounding site: look for an apartment on the first floor or above – a higher level will give you greater exposure to natural light and the energizing effects of *prana*. An apartment block that is square or rectangular will ensure that your home maintains a strong connection with the earth despite its elevated position.

Ideally, look for an apartment on either the north or the east side of the building. Apartment windows in the north or east allow *prana* to enter from the

Despite its modern feel, this conversion adheres to many Vastu guidelines: the room is rectangular in shape; large windows flood the room with light, allowing prana *to enter; the pillars or beams avoid the centre of the room, thereby protecting Vastu Purusha's vulnerable points; and the roof is symmetrically pitched.*

northeast, while other apartments on the floor form a ready-made block, preventing the escape of *prana* in the southwest.

Similar principles apply to terraced housing where end-terraces and those with a garden at the front and the back enjoy the maximum sunlight. Likewise, semi-detached homes that share the south or west wall with their neighbours are better located in terms of energy flow, because the southwest is blocked while the north-east remains clear, allowing *prana* to enter.

The shape of your home

Just as the dimensions of the square provide the perfect shape for the site of your home, this shape is also ideal for both the building itself and individual rooms, with the rectangle an acceptable alternative. If a prospective house is an irregular shape, remember that you may be able to square off an extended corner by adding an extension. With irregularly shaped rooms, consider subdividing the space with screens to create square or rectangular self-contained units. Lesser irregularities are often more easily overcome – for example, an alcove can be turned into a built-in cupboard.

Building materials

Vastu practitioners believe that every substance has a living energy that interacts with our own energy fields, affecting us either positively or negatively. Building materials are therefore thought to affect profoundly the energy dynamics of our homes. Wood, stone and brick have positive effects but reinforced concrete should be avoided if possible – concrete is a lifeless substance and its negative energies are believed to have adverse effects on those living close to it for long periods of time.

The architecture of your home
In terms of esthetics Vastu recommends homes that are visually appealing, with graceful proportions and symmetrical roofs.

Windows are essential to the architectural design of any energized home, as they allow light and therefore *prana* to enter. Consequently, ideal Vastu homes possess an abundance of windows – particularly along the northern and eastern aspects where pranic flow originates.

For similar reasons the best position for a veranda or balcony is along the north or east side of a home where it creates an open space that encourages *prana* to enter. Verandas that run along all four walls should be slightly narrower on the southern and western aspects so that there is proportionately more space in the northeast.

Perfect Vastu staircases are broadly proportioned and constructed from solid materials, such as wood or stone. These characteristics provide a sense of grounding and stability for those ascending the stairs. Preferably, staircases should have an odd number of steps so that we can begin and end the ascent (or descent) on the same foot. (Placing a mat at the bottom of the stairs will create a symbolic extra step for staircases with an even number of steps.) There are also specific Vastu guidelines concerning orientation: ideally, spiral staircases should ascend in a clockwise direction; straight or tapered staircases should ascend from north to south, or from east to west, to facilitate the natural flow of *prana* (from northeast to southwest) up to the upper floors.

Earth resides in the southwest of any home, providing support for the rest of the structure. An underground space (such as a cellar) in this region can undermine such support. Ideally, cellars should either reside in the northeast, or extend along the entire length of the building. (If the cellar is located in the southwest, you will need to fill it with heavy items, such as trunks and boxes, to strengthen the Earth element.)

Decorative structural features

Homes with decorative features are particularly prized in Vastu. These features can be anything from carved architraves to elaborate porches and intricately shaped eaves. According to Vastu such decoration is auspicious because it testifies to the care lavished on the property by the architect. When viewing a home look out for beautiful features that may have become obscured by unsympathetic additions. With plainer homes consider what you might do to enhance or soften the basic structural lines – perhaps with contrasting shades of paint or by introducing vines and creepers.

above *The otherwise simple decoration of this room means attention is drawn to the decorative mouldings on the ceiling and cornices.* **below** *The pillar and raised area in the far southwest corner of the room provide a block that prevents* prana *from escaping.*

 The power of colour

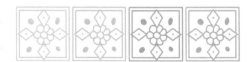

Colour plays an important role in balancing the three *gunas*. It is also central to the creation of a room's atmosphere. You may find that certain colours raise your spirits, and others calm you – like many traditions, Vastu offers a particular explanation for this phenomenon.

Anticipating modern science, ancient Vastu practitioners understood that colours are waves of energy vibrating at specific frequencies to form a spectrum of visible light – or a rainbow. As a dimension of light, every colour that surrounds us has a profound influence on our emotional and spiritual wellbeing. The effects of each colour and the symbolism attached to these in Vastu are summarized opposite.

When the colours of the rainbow come together, white light results. As a combination of all seven wavelengths, white has an especially powerful effect on the senses. Vastu advises against decorating rooms entirely in white, in the belief that individuals will struggle to tolerate its stark brightness for long periods. However, when used in moderation white becomes a handy tool for manipulating energy. For example, if you paint a ceiling white it will reflect light throughout the whole room.

When choosing colours every interior designer – Vastu or otherwise – considers the quality of light in the room. However, Vastu practioners also take into account how the wavelengths of colour that are derived from sunlight vary according to the time of day. If the room that you wish to decorate is in the north or east of the home, it will receive morning sunlight. This predominates in wavelengths from the cooler end of the spectrum: blue, indigo and violet. By contrast, rooms in the south or west of the home receive afternoon and evening sunlight, which mainly contains wavelengths from the warmer end of the spectrum. The quality of the light interacts with the colour tones in each room, impacting upon the overall effect.

This knowledge can be used to modulate or enhance the atmosphere of a room. For example, if a room in the west of your home receives warm evening sunlight, painting the walls in cooler tones will help to modify the warmth of the light. This produces an atmosphere that is calming without being cold. Alternatively, a more exciting effect can be created by enhancing the warmth of the light with hotter tones.

COLOUR	SYMBOLIZES	ATMOSPHERIC EFFECT
Red	Power and bravery	Produces a seductive atmosphere that inflames passion and desire.
Orange	Transcendence	Adds an otherworldly dimension that inspires renunciation and spiritual quest.
Yellow	Sunlight	Supplies a stimulating atmosphere that promotes mental alertness and clarity of mind.
Green	Nature	Creates a harmonious atmosphere that brings calm and inner peace.
Blue	Sky	Gives a sense of space and expansion that relaxes the body and heals the mind.
Indigo	Ocean depths	Adds a sense of depth and mystery that encourages intimacy and revelation.
Violet	Introspection	Encourages a meditative atmosphere that disperses depression and induces positive reflection.

 Personalizing your interior

Like colour, the style of an interior is crucial to the creation of atmosphere. The *rishis* observed that strong esthetic experiences trigger particular moods or mental states. This gave rise to the notion of *rasa*, meaning "taste" or "essence".

According to the Hindu scriptures, there are nine different *rasas*. Three of these are applicable to the interiors of the home. These are *shingara* (the seductive essence), *hasya* (the comic essence) and *sahanta* (the peaceful essence).

The luxury of the *shingara* sentiment is particularly appropriate for living rooms, dining rooms and master bedrooms. To promote this mood, hang richly brocaded fabrics at the windows; scatter embroidered cushions on chairs; and adorn the sacred centre with intricate Persian rugs. For the colour scheme choose a palette of brilliant jewel tones offset by rich earthy hues.

To complement the interior place *shingara* artefacts in the east and north of the room to attract greater wealth and abundance into your life; for example, you can introduce beautifully carved sculptures of the human form, richly coloured paintings depicting an abundance of fruit and flowers, and pictures of cows and elephants – animals that are regarded as sacred in India.

Bold or playful paintings and images, colourful children's toys and similarly kitsch or quirky objects stimulate the *hasya*

rasa and according to Vastu encourage joy when placed anywhere in a room. You can restrict this sentiment to your children's bedrooms, or introduce it into the living and dining rooms to promote lively and stimulating conversation. Decorate a *hasya* room in bright colours, hang cheerful pictures on the walls and use bold printed fabrics for cushions and curtains.

The other *rasa* suitable for the home is *sahanta*. Capture this mood by painting an interior in light, uplifting colours. Limit the use of pattern and ornamentation, which excite the mind. Instead, combine different textures to bring you closer to the tranquillity of nature. Artefacts that complement such interiors – for example, a seated Buddha or other religious icons, and peaceful land- and seascapes – can inspire a sense of contemplative calm. In terms of placement, hang images of water on the north and east walls to increase the flow of *prana* into the room. Images of mountain landscapes will symbolically prevent *prana* escaping from the room if hung on the south or west walls. The southwest quadrant is also the realm of the ancestors, so if you position heirlooms and family photographs in this region you will benefit from their wisdom and support.

following page (from left to right) *Bright, exciting colours combined with a cartoon image and comical model dog evoke* hasya *in this room; passionate shades of pink and red, rich fabrics and an ornate mirror inspire the seductive* shingara rasa; *a Buddha offers a focus for contemplation in a tranquil* sahanta *interior.*

Freeing your space

An important goal of Vastu is to optimize the flow of energy through our homes. During the course of our lives, many of us accumulate an excess of material possessions: outmoded clothes, obsolete household items, unwanted gifts that we feel compelled to keep. These objects clutter up our homes and impede the pranic flow.

According to Vastu clutter in certain areas of the home causes blockages in the corresponding parts of occupants' bodies. For example, unfiled papers in the northeast corner (where Purusha's head is found on the mandala; see pp.20–23) are believed to stifle concentration; piles of junk in the centre of the home, around Purusha's navel, disrupt digestion.

To ensure that *prana* can circulate freely through both your home and body you need to throw out any redundant possessions. In doing so you will symbolically loosen your attachment to the past, allowing you to embrace the future more fully.

First of all take time out to sift through your belongings. Be honest – separate the objects that are truly necessary or meaningful from those you are hoarding for some imagined purpose in the future, or because you cannot let go of the past. Give away or sell any items of value and throw away the rest. Should you have difficulty in parting with certain objects, store them out of sight for a year. After a period of time without missing their presence, you will

An unobtrusive shelving unit provides storage for books, ornaments and other items.

find that you are more able and willing to make the final break.

Of those objects that you decide to keep, select the most beautiful to display in your home. For the remaining objects you need to find simple storage solutions that will keep them out of sight but easily accessible for when you need them. Attics and cellars provide obvious storage spaces but tend to be fairly inaccessible. Fill these spaces with items that you use intermittently. For items that you require more frequently you will have to be more ingenious. Place shelving units for books and music collections in alcoves and under the stairs. Organize your desk with an efficient filing system and get into the habit of filing away your paperwork at least once a week to prevent a build-up.

vastu interiors

CENTRAL TO VASTU IS THE IMPORTANCE OF CREATING AN ATMOS-
PHERE OR MOOD THAT REFLECTS BOTH THE FUNCTION OF A SPACE
AND THE EMOTIONAL AND SPIRITUAL NEEDS OF ITS OCCUPANTS.
ADOPTING A ROOM-BY-ROOM APPROACH, THIS CHAPTER
EXPLORES HOW WE CAN BALANCE THESE DEMANDS IN ORDER
TO CREATE A DEEP SENSE OF HARMONY AND TRANQUILLITY
SPECIFIC TO THE INTERIOR OF EVERY ROOM IN THE HOME, AND TO
THE WORKPLACE. A NUMBER OF DETAILED FLOOR PLANS PRESENT
IDEAL ARRANGEMENTS OF FURNITURE. USING SHAPES, SENSORY
STIMULI AND COLOUR, WE DISCOVER PRACTICAL WAYS TO
CORRECT IMBALANCES OF THE ELEMENTS AND *GUNAS*, AND WE
LEARN THE IMPORTANCE OF INTRODUCING NATURAL ELEMENTS
INTO THE HOME TO HELP US RECONNECT US WITH NATURE.

Thresholds and hallways

In many belief systems thresholds have deep spiritual and symbolic meanings: they mark the transition between one space and another – between civilization and wilderness, pollution and purity, the outer world and the inner world. In Vastu thresholds or doorways play a crucial dual role, allowing positive energy (*prana*) into a space while keeping negative energy at bay. Linking the thresholds, at the core of the home, is the hallway, which distributes incoming *prana* throughout the rest of the structure.

The most significant threshold in any property is the front door. This is the main point of contraflow for incoming and outgoing energies and equates with the mouth of Purusha. Just as the mouth is the largest orifice in the body, the front door should be the largest door in your home. Ensuring that this door is solid will help to protect the home from negative energies. It is best built from a natural material, such as wood.

Indians often position talismans on their front doors to ward off negative influences. Try placing an image or object that represents protection on or by the door to achieve the same effect – a religious icon, such as a cross, perhaps, or, if you would prefer something secular, a statue of a lion.

To attract positive energy into your home, it is important to decorate the front door. Many Indian homes have Lakshmi, the

Light streams into this airy hallway through a well-placed window and decorative openings above the doorway. A beautiful glass bottle refracts green light around the room, welcoming nature into the home.

goddess of wealth and good fortune, carved on the lintel to give blessings as people enter. Strings of marigolds or dried mango leaves tied to the frame represent nature's abundance and attract good luck. Some doorways are inherently decorative, with stained-glass panes and elegant tiled porches. If you have a plain front door, paint it an appealing colour and grow plants in the porch to welcome guests, and *prana*, into the home.

The doors within the home serve as openings that allow *prana* to flow freely throughout the building. It is therefore essential to keep them well-maintained. Each door should sit squarely upon its hinges, opening smoothly and silently without obstruction and, when open, should rest still without swinging shut.

The position of doors in relation to each other plays a significant role in the effective distribution of energy throughout the home. If the back door is in direct alignment with the front door, *prana* will stream straight through the house – in through the front door and out through the back. When the doors to two different rooms face each other across a corridor, energy becomes trapped as it goes in and out of the two rooms in an endless figure of eight. But if the doors are staggered, the energy is able to pass down the corridor, flowing in and out of each individual room as it does so. When two doors are facing one another, place a rug or a hanging mobile between them – this will create a break in the flow that redirects the energy into the remaining rooms of the home.

If the stairs are opposite the front door, incoming energy will travel directly upstairs, bypassing the downstairs rooms. However, some of this energy can be deflected down the stairs to the rest of the house by placing a mirror at the top of the first flight of stairs (opposite the front door).

Light is a source of *prana*, so the hallway should receive as much light as possible. If your hallway is dark, install ample lighting and paint it a sattvic (pale) colour such as cream (the *sattva guna* encourages *prana* to enter a space).

A prominent mirror introduces Water into this hallway – Water is a restless element that is well-suited to this type of transitional space. The decorative tiled floor welcomes positive energy into the home.

The living room

Of all the rooms in the home, the living room is where we tend to spend most time relaxing. In Vastu this space is regarded as the nucleus of our living environment – a place for private pursuits, such as reading, as well as for communal, interactive activities, such as entertaining. Accordingly, the living room should extend into the centre of the home – toward the heart of Purusha – where, in Indian houses, there is often an open courtyard.

Although most houses do not have a central courtyard, a similar atmosphere can be created by thinking of your living room as the symbolic centre of your home, a place where family and friends can gather to enjoy each other's company. Recognize the importance of this nucleus by keeping the middle of the room free from clutter.

Ideally, the living room should be located in the north, west or northwest of the house. The north is guarded by Kubera, god of wealth, whose presence in a room creates an auspicious ambience. West and northwest living rooms receive the rays of the setting sun – as most of us spend our evenings in the living room, both locations are ideal in terms of maximizing our daily exposure to sunlight and *prana*.

The level of activity in the living room reinforces the northwest as a good location. The Air and Water elements and the

The textures of the brick walls and warm wooden floors in this living room promote the Air element, making it an ideal space for sociable activity and evening entertainment.

restless *rajas guna* reside there, encouraging energetic movement through the space.

If your living room is situated elsewhere in your home, there are many techniques you can use to bring the positive qualities of a north, west or northwest placement into the room. You can simulate the effects of evening light by choosing a colour scheme with accents of warmer hues: creams tinged with yellow, blues flushed with rosy pink. Stimulate *rajas* by introducing potent flashes of fiery colour into the details of your interior. Hang a mirror on the wall to encourage Water, and have a mix of textures in your furnishings to promote Air. Often treated routinely,

flooring offers wonderful opportunities for experimenting with textures. For example, try rough-hewn sisal or seagrass matting, or a contrast between fluffy rugs and the smooth grain of varnished floorboards.

Remember that while you are trying to bring qualities of the west and northwest into your living room, you should also appease its "resident" elements and *gunas* – that is, the elements and *gunas* that *are* present in the space. If your living room is in the southwest, a bowl of stones will help to appease Earth. In the southeast lighted candles will pacify Fire; and in the northeast reducing clutter will satisfy Ether. Similarly, to balance the *gunas*, introduce

left *Textured cushions stimulate Air.* **right** *The orange colour of this mosaic symbolizes transcendence and is the ideal adornment for the sacred centre of a living room where Brahma sits.*

dark tamasic colours into the furnishings of southwestern living rooms, with lighter sattvic shades for those in the northeast.

The position of your furniture in the living room – indeed, in any room – is critical to ensuring that *prana* is encouraged to flow freely. The largest pieces of furniture in this area are likely to be the sofa and chairs, as well as perhaps shelving for books and music. Place these items in the southwest of the room where, supported by Earth and its predominant *guna tamas*, they can serve as a block that prevents *prana* from escaping. If possible, place your chairs or sofa along the south wall, so that those sitting down are facing north. In

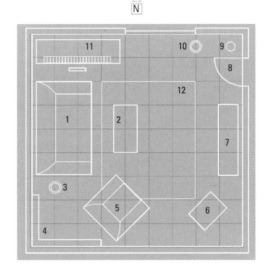

1 sofa	7 fireplace
2 coffee table	8 door
3 tall plant	9 lamp
4 bookshelf	10 flowering plant
5 armchair	11 piano
6 television/hi-fi	12 rug

A vibrant yellow flower (above right) or scarlet cushion (below right) will stimulate rajas, and a mirror (above left) will encourage Water. In southwest living rooms small stones (below left) will appease Earth.

Vastu this direction is known as *Kubera sthana* and bestows wealth and power on those who face it.

Modern Vastu practitioners equate electrical equipment, such as the television and stereo system, with Fire. For this reason these items should be located in the southeast Fire corner. Place them in glass, metal or stone units, which can contain Fire. This is particularly important if your electrical equipment is stored elsewhere in the room, in conflict with other elements.

Keep games and musical instruments in the northwest corner of the room. This area is governed by the Air and Water elements, and is ideal for challenging pursuits.

A simple way of harnessing the many benefits of Vastu in your living room is to turn the northeast corner (where Ether resides) into a "zone of tranquillity". By keeping this area as clear as possible, *prana* is able to enter the room freely. Scatter a few floor cushions here, and perhaps create a discreet altar with some candles and a Buddha statue (or other inspirational image). Treat this space as contemplative – spend a few quiet moments in meditation here each day, or, if there is room, use it to practise simple yoga postures or t'ai chi. Traditionally, such practices were undertaken facing east, in the direction of the rising sun (a symbol of inner illumination).

A mirror on the wall represents the element Water, while the reds and pinks of cushions and flowers stimulate rajas. A Buddha in the northeastern corner provides the focal point for a "zone of tranquillity".

The kitchen

Indians believe that two main sources of *prana* sustain the body: the air that we breathe and the food that we eat. The kitchen is therefore one of the most important areas of the home, for it is here that we prepare food.

According to Ayurveda (the Indian system of holistic medicine), the process of cooking renders food more digestible, unlocking its stores of *prana* for our bodies' consumption. To cook food properly we need an abundance of the Fire element, which is found primarily in the southeast of the home – the ideal location for a kitchen.

Like the southeast, the northwest is animated by the *rajas guna* – a restless energy well-suited to the bustle of the kitchen. The northwest is therefore an acceptable alternative site for the kitchen. There is a risk that the resident Water element will interfere with the cooking by extinguishing Fire (ruler of the kitchen). To combat this effect you can strengthen Fire by stimulating sight with vivid spices and pickles displayed on shelves.

Kitchens in other parts of the home require greater effort to balance their energies. The inertia of *tamas* in kitchens sited in the southwest tends to drain the energy from foods that are prepared there. Incorporating warm rajasic colours into the decor will mitigate this effect. Try laying

Colourful jars of pickles appeal to the senses of sight and taste, stimulating both Fire and Water respectively, and thereby helping to keep these conflicting elements in balance.

terracotta flagstones on the floor, patterning the walls with colourful tiles, or simply displaying oranges and lemons in a bowl.

Kitchens in the northeast call for the opposite approach. Purusha's head lies in the northeast, so bringing Fire into this region may cause headaches and arguments among its occupants. In such kitchens avoid wooden units, which will feed the flames. Instead, install metal or stone units to contain the Fire and protect Purusha's head.

Within any kitchen there is always a conflict between Fire and Water. For this reason the cooker and the sink should be separated – either by placing a work surface between them or, better still, by arranging them in an L-shape with the sink along the north wall (near the Water element) and the cooker in the east. The sun rises in the east and, as a source of *prana*, makes this direction rich in vitality and the power of growth. According to Vastu these positive energies will infuse your food if you face east as you cook.

Food soaks up the energies of the chef. To ensure that you are relaxed when cooking, make the effort to create a well-organized and pleasant kitchen. Fitted kitchens, with their specially designed storage units, provide good solutions to any organizational problems. Arrange your

The red painted drawers of the central table stimulate the restless energy of rajas, *the* guna *most appropriate for the excitement and activity of the kitchen.*

store cupboards so that the heaviest are positioned along the south and west walls of the kitchen, where they are supported by the Earth element.

Vastu associates food with wealth and abundance, so keeping a well-stocked fridge is one way to ensure prosperity. However, a build-up of discarded or rotting food not only breeds harmful bacteria, but also inhibits the free flow of *prana* through the space. Above all, therefore, it is vital to keep your kitchen clean, and stocked as far as possible with the freshest ingredients. Also ensure that it is well-ventilated – this will prevent cooking odours from permeating the rest of the home.

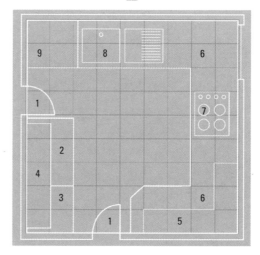

1	door	6	storage cupboards
2	breakfast bar	7	cooker
3	fridge/freezer	8	sink
4	wall-mounted shelves	9	washer/dryer
5	wall-mounted cupboards		

left *Ripe, rosy pears stimulate the senses of sight and taste, encouraging the elements of Fire and Water respectively.* **right** *Stacking crockery neatly on shelves reduces clutter, thereby aiding the pranic flow.*

The dining room

According to ayurvedic medicine, the key to wellbeing is good digestion. This is affected not only by what we eat, but also by the manner and atmosphere in which we eat. Faced with the time pressures of modern living, we tend to place mealtimes low on our list of priorities: lunchtime is a cursory affair – a sandwich eaten on the run, or at a desk; dinner is consumed in front of the television, or over a book.

When we eat quickly, without savouring our meal and chewing slowly, we hamper our body's ability to digest the food properly. This limits the nutritional benefits of the meal, and, according to ayurvedic practitioners, produces a toxic substance called *ama*, which lies at the root of all illness. To counteract these damaging effects, it is important that – in the home at least – our dining experiences be relaxed and comfortable, ensuring healthy digestion and full enjoyment of the food.

In contrast to the bustle of the kitchen, a dining room should be restful and re-energizing. Try to maintain a clear distinction between kitchen activity and relaxed dining by keeping the two rooms separate. If your dining area is within the kitchen, try to establish a clear delineation between the two areas – a partition, such

Soft cream walls induce a sense of calm and supply an appropriate backdrop for a variety of dining occasions. A rectangular wooden table surrounded by wooden chairs connects diners with the Earth element – providing a sense of comfort and security as they eat.

as a breakfast bar or counter, is ideal. Alternatively, lay different types of flooring or place a rug beneath the table and chairs. If such obvious definition is not practicable, use lighting to mark out the two areas. Install dimmable spotlights on two different circuits, or, more simply, turn off the kitchen lights and illuminate the dining table with candles during the meal.

If you do not have a separate dining room, the living room offers a more restful space for dining than the kitchen. Form an eating area by dividing the space with folding screens, large plants or a piece of furniture such as a freestanding bookcase.

Whether you are eating in the kitchen, the living room or a separate dining room, the best location is toward the west of a room or home, where the setting sun creates the perfect atmosphere for evening meals. The east provides an alternative location, although this is more suitable for breakfast when you can greet the rising sun over a reviving morning drink.

Within any dining area the most important furnishings are the table and chairs. As a bearer of nourishment, your dining table should be either square or rectangular to represent Earth. Round or oval tables symbolize Water, an element that,

above left *Scarlet flowers can kindle desire over a romantic dinner.* above right *Candles improve appetite by stimulating Fire.* below left *Citrus fruits stimulate taste, thereby strengthening Water, which resides in the west.* below right *Wooden-handled cutlery and linen napkins bring natural elements into the dining room.*

according to Vastu, can induce restlessness in diners. (This can make it difficult to gather people for meals, and bring dinner parties to a premature close, with guests anxious to leave.)

To "earth" your diners as they eat, choose either a wooden table, or a glass or ceramic-tiled table with a wooden base. For the same reason, wooden dining chairs are also preferable. These should be comfortable, with supportive backs to encourage good posture, thereby easing digestion.

Fundamental to Vastu is the alignment of your dining table, which should be oriented according to the four cardinal directions. The chairs should be positioned so that diners face either east to ensure longevity, or west to invite prosperity. For example, if you have a rectangular table, the long sides should align along a north–south axis, so that chairs can be placed down either side facing east and west. Even if you have an odd number of guests, place an even number of chairs around the table – according to Vastu this will bring good fortune to the household.

The atmosphere that you wish to create in your dining room will depend largely on the occasion. Paint the walls in calming blues, greens or soft creams – these colours

above *The relaxing colours of the blue walls and a green dresser provide the perfect backdrop for dining.*
opposite *In this dining room various features encourage Fire, thereby stimulating digestion: flickering candle flames, beautiful flower arrangements, and the triangular shape of the candle holder – a symbol of Fire.*

will provide a suitable backdrop for any dining situation. Vary the colours of napkins, placemats and tableware to conjure your desired atmosphere: inspire profound and intimate conversation between friends with hints of dark tamasic indigo; stimulate cheerful, witty banter at family gatherings with flashes of brilliant rajasic yellow.

These colours can also be incorporated into elegant table arrangements of flowers, fruit and candles, which enhance the general atmosphere of the room: the gentle, hypnotic flicker of candle flames pacifies the mind and promotes relaxation; the visual beauty of the arrangements activates sight and thereby stimulates the Fire element. In this way these arrangements improve our absorption of food because, in Vastu, Fire is essential for good digestion.

The study

As the boundaries between our professional and personal lives merge, we often need an area at home in which to work. However, according to Vastu bringing the active energies of the workplace into the calm oasis of the home provokes conflict – with the result that we can neither concentrate on our work, nor ever truly relax. So how can we overcome this dilemma?

Ideally, dedicate a specific room to your work so that in the evening you can close the door on the day's activities and preserve the tranquillity of your home. If space is limited and your workstation has to occupy another room of the home, use shelving or screens to create a work area in a room that is used infrequently, such as the guest room, or in a place of diverse energies, such as the living room.

The position of your study can have a profound influence on your ability to work effectively. Generally, try to minimize distractions from incoming and outgoing energies by locating your study far from the front door. More specifically, different types of work benefit from the properties of different locations. If you have a research-based or creative job, aim to position your study in the north where Ether will expand your mind, and Air and Water will promote fresh ideas. (Alternatively, try stimulating your senses to encourage these elements: soothing sounds will promote Ether; the textured weave of a basket of luscious oranges will strengthen Air and Water.)

If you work in the commercial sectors, you would benefit from a southwest location where you will be supported by Earth. (If you cannot locate your study in this area, you can strengthen Earth through smell by burning essential oils, or arranging a vase of fragrant flowers on your desk.)

The placement of the desk in your study is particularly important. The southwest corner is the optimum location for it because this is the home of the Earth element, which can support heavy furniture. Orient the desk so that, when sitting, you face either east or north: the east will inspire new and innovative ideas; the north will expand your knowledge.

Flowers displayed on the desk attract prana to the workstation and stimulate the supportive Earth element. Wooden shelving provides ample storage space for files so that clutter does not impede the pranic flow.

If you are experiencing a confidence crisis in your work, ensure that you are not sitting with your back to any doors or windows – according to Vastu this can produce feelings of insecurity. If you cannot move your desk to another position, try at least to have it square or rectangular in shape and built from solid wood – this will inspire Earth in your workspace, helping you to feel more grounded.

If you find it hard to concentrate, check that your desk is not made from metal or glass. The conductive properties of these materials can spark disruptive energy patterns. Either replace the existing desk with a wooden one, or stand a plant by your desk. As well as "earthing" the wayward energy, the plant will absorb the radiation from your computer.

Ideally, all electrical items should be located apart from your main working area, in the southeast (Fire) corner of the room. In practice, computers often form the centrepieces of desks because they are the main focus of the work. To compromise, place your computer toward the southeast of your desk, and keep a plant nearby.

Many people spend a good proportion of their working time sitting. In Indian philosophy the way we sit affects our general energy levels and ability to work: bad posture impedes the flow of *prana* through the

Walls painted in pale shades promote sattva *which brings calmness of mind and clarity of thought. Hints of warm rajasic red in the floor and fabrics excite the mind, enhancing productivity.*

sushumna nadi – the energy channel believed to run up the middle of the spine – distributing energy to the various parts of our body. A comfortable, well-proportioned chair that you can adjust to suit your individual physiological requirements can help to improve your posture (and hence the flow of *prana* through your body).

Above all, it is important to treat your study area as your own personal space, a place in which to concentrate away from the distractions of the home. Put a meaningful image in the northeast of your study to form the centrepiece of a "zone of tranquillity" that will focus and inspire your mind. When choosing wall colours consider the energy that you wish to promote: blue invokes expansion, encouraging higher thought; yellow is mentally stimulating.

The bathroom

The bathroom is the natural home of Water, the element deemed sacred for its powers to cleanse and purify mind, body and spirit. For this reason it has always played a vital role in religious rituals – in India devotees of Hinduism bathe in the holy waters of temples or in sacred rivers, such as the Ganges, to repel harmful spirits and cleanse themselves of past misdeeds. Within our homes we should view the bathroom as a similarly sacred space, for it is here that we tend to the temple of the soul, cleansing the body and purifying the mind.

Traditional Indian homes position the bathroom and toilet (which are usually separated) away from the main house. This keeps the bathroom pure and ensures that waste products do not contaminate the home. However, in the majority of Western homes the bathroom is found within the main building, so we need to achieve the Vastu ideal using placement technique.

The northwest is the most obvious location for any bathroom because it is ruled by the element Water. If there is no toilet in your bathroom, the east offers a good alternative (if you have a toilet in the east of the home, *prana* entering at the northeast will drain away through the plumbing). In an eastern bathroom that has

The ruling Water element and resident Fire element are brought into harmonious balance in this southeastern bathroom – an abundance of mirrors and shiny surfaces encourage the Water element, while the flames of lighted candles represent the Fire element.

windows, you will be blessed by the beneficial rays of morning sunlight as you take your morning shower or bath.

On the other hand, if your bathroom includes a toilet, the best position is near the genital area of Vastu Purusha in the southwest of the home, close to the master bedroom. However, try to avoid en suite bathrooms: while these are acceptable for short-term usage (as in hotel rooms), in permanent residential properties they create a conflict between the divergent energies of bathroom and bedroom. If you already have an en suite bathroom, or a bathing area within the bedroom, separate the conflicting energies with a closed door, or some form of curtain or screen.

Homes that have the bathroom in the southeast suffer from an elemental imbalance, as the Water element (which rules the bathroom) extinguishes the Fire element (which governs the southeast of the home). To counter these effects it is important to stimulate Fire in the bathroom. Try lighting some candles; these literally emphasize Fire and have the added benefit of creating a meditative atmosphere that will soothe you as you bathe. Arrange some red flowers in a beautiful vase to add a splash of fiery rajasic colour to the room, or

left *A loofah brings a natural element into the bathroom.* right *Flowers stimulate sight and therefore activate Fire. Place them next to a mirror (Water) to bring Fire and Water into harmony in southeastern bathrooms.*

hang a beautiful picture on the wall to stimulate sight (the sense linked with Fire).

If the bathroom is in the northeast, incoming *prana* will drain away through the plumbing system. If a northeastern location is your only option, make sure that the bathroom is as light and spacious as possible. Keep the door open when the room is unoccupied to allow *prana* to flow into the rest of the home, and close the toilet lid when it is not in use to prevent *prana* escaping through the pipes.

The layout of the bathroom can also help to regulate pranic flow. The bulkiest items in the bathroom tend to be the bath and shower units, and the storage cupboards for towels and other bathroom supplies; position these along the south or west walls to prevent *prana* escaping. Fix your medicine cabinet on the north wall. This aspect is ruled by Kubera, the god of wealth, who is also believed to possess healing powers because he resides in the Himalaya, where many of the ayurvedic medicinal herbs grow. Install the basin along either the north or east wall, but not in the northeast corner where *prana* enters the room. The orientation of the toilet can prove problematic; ideally, you should face north when sitting, so the toilet should be aligned on a north–south axis without facing the door directly or being too close to the window.

As the bathroom is a place for purification and rejuvenation, it should be kept scrupulously clean. An extractor fan prevents mildew and removes any unpleasant odours, while essential oils or potpourri

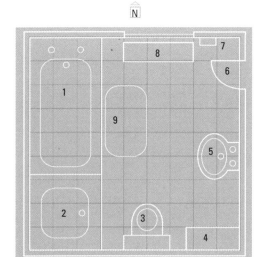

1 bath	6 door
2 shower	7 medicine cabinet
3 toilet	8 low storage cupboards
4 boiler	9 bath mat
5 basin/mirror	

light, refreshing colours such as off-white, pale blue or green and laying the floor with watery-coloured tiles or even marble slabs.

To encourage Water (the element that governs the activity of bathing) install an abundance of reflective surfaces such as mirrors and gleaming tiles. Alternatively, you could evoke watery environments with stunning tiled mosaics, exquisite shells, starfish and natural sponges.

Appropriate lighting is important for creating the right atmosphere in the bathroom. Dimmable spotlights are ideal: in the morning you can turn them up to full brightness to awaken your mind in readiness for the activities of the day; in the evening you can dim them to create a more subdued and relaxing atmosphere suitable for a leisurely evening soak.

freshen the air without the need for over-powering synthetic aerosol sprays. Enhance the pure atmosphere by painting the walls

The master bedroom

Bedrooms should provide us with sanctuary from the pressures of daily living. In the ancient yoga scriptures, sleep is described as a blissful state in which we reunite with the peaceful essence of our true nature. Good-quality sleep is indeed vital for our wellbeing, and creating the right bedroom environment is essential for achieving this.

According to Vastu, feeling secure in our bedroom environment is necessary for restful sleep. In homes where there is more than one floor, bedrooms located on the first floor, or higher, immediately give a sense of protection from the outside world.

In most homes the master bedroom is occupied by the principal adults of the house and should therefore be the largest of the bedrooms. The southwest quadrant of the home, guarded by Nirtti (the nocturnal god of sleep and demons), is the ideal location. In this region the Earth element provides a secure environment for relaxation, while the inert energy of *tamas* induces the torpor of deep sleep. Where there are windows in the west, the room also receives the warm rays of the setting sun – the perfect soothing accompaniment to bedtime rituals.

The ornate wooden four-poster bedframe and delicately draped mosquito net create a safe yet romantic haven in which to sleep. An adjacent window brings openness to the room by day, while the shutters keep light at bay during hours of sleep. The dark brown wood and chestnut-coloured cushion enhance the tamasic energies of the interior, while delightfully scented flowers stimulate smell and therefore Earth.

If you cannot locate your bedroom in the south or southwest, the north offers an alternative. Try to avoid the southeast or northwest because the predominant rajasic energies induce a restlessness that inhibits sleep. If you have no choice, boost the rooting qualities of Earth and *tamas* by placing a bowl of natural stones by the bed, burning incense or essential oils to stimulate your sense of smell, and introducing dark tamasic tints into the colour scheme.

Once you have determined the location of the master bedroom, the furniture should be positioned to enhance the pranic flow. As the bed is generally the largest object in any bedroom, place it in the southwest of the room to help prevent *prana* from escaping. According to Vastu, because the body produces an electromagnetic field it possesses the characteristics of a magnet, with the head as the north pole. To ensure restful sleep it is important to orient the body according to the electromagnetic field of the Earth. As opposite poles attract, position your bed so that your head points toward the south wall. If you sleep with your head pointing north, the north pole of your head will repel that of the Earth, causing energy disturbances that will disrupt sleep.

Where there is space, arrange your storage cupboards along the south or west

In this bedroom green brings a calmness and tranquillity that is conducive to sleep, while sumptuous fabrics add a more seductive dimension.

walls to prevent *prana* escaping from the room. If this is impossible, the north or east walls offer an alternative, provided that you keep the northeast corner of the room clear to allow *prana* to enter freely.

Jewelry and other valuables should be kept in the northern aspect of your bedroom where they will be guarded by Kubera, the god of wealth.

Ideally, the design of your bedroom should enhance your rest. Choosing a wooden frame for your bed will connect you to the Earth element, providing the security that is needed for peaceful sleep. (Try to avoid metal-framed beds – their

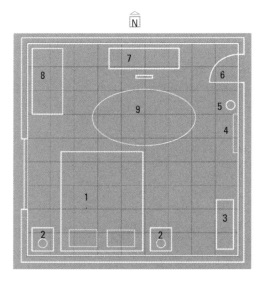

1 bed
2 bedside table
3 chest of drawers
4 mirror
5 freestanding lamp
6 door
7 dressing table
8 wardrobe
9 rug

above *Fitted cupboards surrounding the bed mean that even in a small room all the heavy items of furniture are located in the south or west quadrants.* **below** *An injection of bright pink into this otherwise muted and minimal interior helps to create an atmosphere of passion.*

conductive powers produce negative patterns of energy around the body, causing physical stress and sleep disturbances.) In terms of proportions, an ideal Vastu bed is 4ft 6in (1.35m) wide. However, as long as there is sufficient space to move easily around your bedroom (allowing *prana* to circulate), any size of bed is acceptable.

The fabric of your sheets can also affect the quality of your sleep. Natural fibres such as cotton, linen or silk are best – they will keep you warm, while allowing your skin to breathe. By contrast, polyester sheets can give rise to static electricity and cause uncomfortable sweating.

Our sleeping patterns are governed by levels of sunlight. A flexible lighting scheme that combines dimmable uplighters or overhead spots with low-wattage reading lamps allows us to mimic the changing brightness of the sun and so regulate our sleeping patterns: dimming the lights in the evening prepares the mind for rest; increasing the brightness gradually in the morning provides a gentle awakening to the day.

Choose your colour scheme according to the atmosphere that you wish to promote: soft shades of red stimulate passion; delicate shades of green or blue produce a calm and soothing environment.

above left *The fragrance of potpourri stimulates the sense of smell and therefore Earth.* **above right** *These luxurious blankets are made from the natural fibres of mohair and silk.* **below left** *Square-shaped cushions represent Earth.* **below right** *Freshly cut flowers attract* prana *to the bedside, promoting energizing sleep.*

The children's bedroom

A child's bedroom should not only provide a safe, stable and personalized environment but should also stimulate the imagination and arouse curiosity.

Children under ten years old tend to sleep best in the east of the home. Here they become attuned to the cycle of the sun – arising at dawn and settling down at dusk. (A newborn who shares the master bedroom should have his or her cot in the east of the room.)

If your child is prone to fretful crying or temper tantrums, check whether his or

her bedroom is located in the southeast of the house, where the Fire element can cause friction and restlessness. If you find this to be the case, incorporate something that represents the Water element, such as a mirror, into the room – this will help to dampen the flames of Fire.

Teenage children are believed to sleep well in any cardinal direction. However, try to avoid the southwest where they may feel weighed down by responsibility, or even attempt to dominate the household. The north is a particularly beneficial

Bright glass panels set into the rajasic orange wall stimulate interest and excitement for young children. Through the doorway a separate sleeping area ensures that playthings can be shut away at bedtime.

position, as this is the direction from which we acquire knowledge.

Suitable design schemes for younger children combine sattvic (pale, calming) colours, to promote growth, with rajasic (warm, exciting) colours to stimulate the imagination. Allow older children to decorate their own rooms – it is important that they define their own space, developing an individual taste and identity.

Whether your children are toddlers or teenagers, position their beds against the south wall toward the southwest corner, so that their heads point southward when they sleep. In the north or east of the room, if there is space, create an activity or work area with a desk or table. Children are better able to make clear distinctions between work and play than adults, so this should

not disrupt their sleep patterns. However, try to keep electrical equipment away from the bedroom because the positive ions that it produces will disturb sleep. This rule may be impossible to enforce with teenagers – compromise by putting the equipment in the southeast of the room in a glass or metal cabinet that can be closed at night.

Children tend to accumulate a large amount of possessions, so it is important to provide effective storage space to keep *prana* flowing freely. For young children install low shelving in the northwest of the room for toys and games. For older ones, cupboards along the west wall will furnish ample space for teenage clutter.

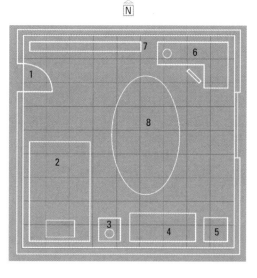

1. door
2. bed
3. bedside table
4. wardrobe
5. hi-fi
6. desk
7. shelves
8. rug

Textures stimulate Air (associated with movement), and pale walls enhance sattva *(representing growth and expansion). These qualities create a suitable environment for teenagers soon to enter into adulthood.*

The guest room

The guest room is a place of transience – a space where people come and go like the ebb and flow of water, or the gentle movement of air.

When you bear this in mind, the northwest of your home presents the best location for any guest room. Here the restless elements of Air and Water complement the transitory nature of the room, instead of unsettling permanent residents.

When positioning the furniture follow the rules that apply to the master bedroom: create space in the northeast to allow *prana* to enter freely, and keep the bed and other heavy furniture along the south and west walls to contain the *prana*. If your guest room is located in an area other than the northwest, compromise by placing the bed along the west wall, close to the restless northwest corner.

Providing an en suite bathroom for the guest room, or more simply a basin in the corner of the room, will give both you and your guests greater privacy. In this instance Vastu permits the mixing of sleeping and bathing energies within one room because the guest room is used only for short periods of time. Locate the en suite bathroom or basin in the northwest Water corner. If this is not possible, position a mirror over the basin to stimulate Water in that region instead.

The neutral tones of this bedroom will not affront any visitor. The circular shape of the table introduces Water, a restless element well-suited to the transitory character of the guest room.

Decorate the guest room in soft, neutral colours to suit any taste, and keep pictures and ornaments to a minimum. By making sure that the design is simple and unobtrusive, you will create a space in which people can relax. A vase of fresh flowers by the bedside will help your visitors to feel wanted and welcome, the aromatic scent grounding them during their stay by introducing Earth into the room.

When not in regular use, the guest room can all too easily become a dumping ground for household junk, particularly if it doubles as the venue for activities such as exercise or music practice. Install effective storage (preferably in the southwest of the room to create a block that stops *prana* escaping), so that clutter can be cleared away and your guests have ample space.

Open-plan living spaces: lofts and studios

As former warehouses and factories on urban fringes are converted into trendy studio and loft apartments, open-plan living has become increasingly popular among city dwellers. In Vastu terms these homes provide wonderfully light, airy and energized places in which to live, because the absence of dividing walls means that *prana* can flow freely throughout.

Within an open-plan living space, the distribution of functions should mirror that of any Vastu home. The bathing and sleeping areas benefit from the properties of Water and Earth in the west and southwest of the home respectively. The greater activity of the general living area suits the rajasic restlessness of Air and Water in the northwest quadrant. Cooking and preparing food require the Fire of the southeast corner, while an eating area near a window in the east benefits from the rays of morning sunlight at breakfast. The northeast channels *prana* into the home and is the perfect place for a study or quiet meditation and yoga corner. To overcome problems of layout, follow the advice given for individual rooms. This will show you how to use objects and design to balance the elements and *gunas* according to the demands of particular functions and locations.

A wall of windows imparts the lightness and airiness typical of many open-plan apartments. Different areas are clearly separated with varying types of stone, tiled and wooden flooring, combined with small groups of furniture and a freestanding wall.

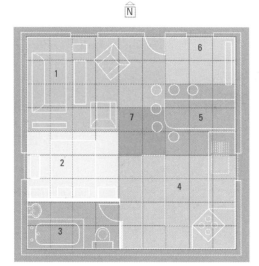

N

1 living area
2 sleeping area
3 bathroom
4 kitchen area
5 dining area
6 study/meditation area
7 open centre

To avoid the risk of conflict between the divergent energies of the different zones, it is crucial to establish a clear demarcation between them. A good start is to obtain some freestanding screens. Their mobility will give you the flexibility to divide your home or open it up as occasion demands – you can enjoy the benefits of an expanded vista while working during the day, then screen off your desk at night. Paper or rattan screens hanging from the ceiling, or panels on sliding tracks, are more permanent solutions. More simply, you can arrange your existing furniture – such as freestanding bookcases, sofas, or armchairs

The high ceiling of this apartment permits a raised bed. This establishes a separation of the living and sleeping areas while retaining the openness of the space. Elsewhere in the room a selection of rugs beneath groups of furniture define specific areas, and a rug kept clear in the middle marks the sacred centre.

– into small groups to create self-contained areas. Yet another (more permanent) approach is to use different colours or types of flooring to separate off individual zones (this technique will also help to preserve the openness of one-room living). You could paint your meditation area a calming green and lay a wooden floor on which to practise yoga; or tile your kitchen area in fiery reds and warm yellows, with flagstones for the floor.

Whatever the size of your apartment, incorporate effective storage systems and multifunctional furniture to keep disorder and clutter to a minimum. This will ensure that you preserve the pranic flow and natural airiness of your open-plan home.

The bed is one of the hardest pieces of furniture to integrate into a studio because

its size can dominate the space. If you have a high ceiling, building an elevated bed will instantly alleviate this problem. A futon or sofa bed will also present an instant fix, although clearing away the bedding each day can become a chore. (If you do use a futon or sofa bed, ensure that it is one intended for daily use.) A simpler solution might be to position your bed lengthways along a wall and strew it with cushions. By this ploy it will seem less out of keeping in your living space and will also provide additional seating.

A fitted kitchen is invaluable in an open-plan home, not least because it offers well-organized cupboard space for utensils and ingredients. Suspend a rack from the ceiling on which to hang pots and pans out of the way, and install a hinged or pull-out kitchen table to create an additional work- or eating surface. An efficient extractor fan will ensure that stale cooking smells do not permeate the entire living space.

The most important areas to keep clear are the northeast section through which *prana* enters, and the sacred centre where Brahma sits. Adorn the latter with a rug – this will remind you to keep the space clear, and will also encourage you to revere this sacred area.

above left *Playing the piano is an activity suited to the restless energies of the northwest.* **above right** *An eastern dining area receives sunlight at breakfast time.* **below left** *Tamasic (grounding) brown leather chairs bring balancing stillness to the living area.* **below right** *A Buddha is the focus for a meditation corner.*

Vastu in the workplace

As we have seen, our home environment has a profound influence on our health, happiness and general prosperity. Our work environment, where many of us spend a large proportion of our waking lives, has a similar impact. If we follow the principles of Vastu, we can transform our workplaces into sources of inspiration and creativity, encouraging an atmosphere of industry and vitality in which employers and employees alike feel valued and motivated.

In terms of general layout, the northeast of an office building is the optimum location for the reception – the interface between the office and the outside world, a channel for visitors and *prana* alike. The reception desk should be placed toward the southwest corner of the reception area where it is supported by Earth. Orient the desk so that the receptionist faces the doorway and is able to greet any visitors upon their arrival.

The northeast is also ideal for workers occupied in any sort of creative activity. Here they will gain inspiration from incoming *prana*, and their minds will be calmed and cleared by Ether. At the same time workers positioned in this region should also encourage the Earth element, which will provide them with support, and inject practicality into radical, new ideas. We can achieve this by placing a potted plant, or some other natural element, on our desks.

The southeast of an office building is the best location for a communal kitchen, or cafeteria. In this area the resident Fire element provides the heat necessary for the cooking and good digestion of food.

Electrical equipment, such as faxes and photocopiers, should also be placed in the southeast of the building because modern Vastu equates electricity with Fire. However, as it is impractical to keep all electrical items in a single area of the building, compromise by grouping them in the southeast corners of individual areas.

In addition to Fire the southeast is dominated by *rajas*. For administrative workers this combination of energies is beneficial because it promotes efficiency. However, for other workers in the southeast a predominance of *rajas* and Fire can spark friction, lowering irritation thresholds and exacerbating tempers.

Encourage *tamas* into the southeastern area to ease any tensions. This is an inert energy, which promotes reliability and tolerance. Place a plant with dark, dense leaves to the southwest of your desk, or incorporate dark colours, such as indigo and charcoal, into the design of your workspace (for example, in the colours of lamps and seat covers). If the company is investing in new desks, ask for ones built from heavy, tamasic woods, or in dark colours.

In the southwest quadrant of an office building, Earth provides support and stability. This creates a favourable working environment for those in managerial roles who require additional confidence for leading others. Those working in this area also receive the benefits of a strong connection with ancestral wisdom, which is invaluable for making difficult decisions. This is provided by Yama, the Vedic god of the dead, who presides in the south.

In terms of the *gunas*, the southwest of an office is dominated by *tamas*. When in excess, this energy can engender tendencies toward sluggishness and mental fatigue. If your desk is located in this area, a hint of fiery rajasic colour can do much to banish such lethargy: when given the choice, opt for brightly coloured office equipment – perhaps a red mousemat or file rack, or even a neon-pink computer monitor. Alternatively, arrange some red or yellow flowers in a vase in the southeast or northwest (rajasic) corner of your desk.

If your office is in the southwest, it is also important to encourage Ether. This element will open your mind to more creative and progressive approaches to your work. To stimulate Ether, banish piles of clutter, such as the paper and correspondence that typically build up in an office. By clearing more space (particularly in the northeast of your desk) you will create room in which to work, and allow *prana* to flow more easily.

In the northwest quadrant of a building, Water, Air and *rajas* predominate, giving rise to an atmosphere of transience that is ideal for conference facilities or temporary workers. However, permanent staff positioned in the northwest of an office may be unsettled by these restless energies, experiencing problems with concentration, as well as a tendency toward impracticality and unreliability.

To mitigate such negative effects, it is important to encourage the rooting qualities of Earth and the clarity of *sattva*. As before, place a plant in the southwest of your desk area to stimulate Earth. To

promote *sattva* you will need to introduce some cool, pale colours into your workstation. The simplest way is to arrange a vase of sattvic (pale and delicate) flowers on your desk – perhaps some arum lilies or a spray of jasmine. Alternatively, if you are feeling bold, why not make a point of, or suggest, including these colours when the office decor is being revamped?

In general, it is important to keep the centre of an office building as open as possible. This area represents the heart of the company and any clutter will impede the smooth running of the business. Such a central space could take the form of a spectacular glass atrium or courtyard, or in more modest buildings, perhaps an open lounge where workers from different departments can congregate and converse.

In terms of the arrangement of furniture, the best strategy for open-plan offices is to position desks around the edges of each section, leaving clear spaces in the centre that protect the vulnerable points of Purusha. In self-contained offices the general Vastu principles of room layout are applicable: place the desk in the southwest, and keep the northeast and sacred centre free to allow *prana* to flow freely.

Whether you have a self-contained room, or work in an open-plan office, it is important to enhance the flow of *prana* with adequate lighting. Fluorescent strip lights tend to deplete the energy of those working under them. Ideally, supplement natural light with full-spectrum lamps positioned in the northeast of each desk to promote the flow of *prana*.

sacred nature

VASTU CAN BE APPLIED TO ANY OUTDOOR SPACE, WHETHER IT IS A GARDEN, DECK, PATIO OR BALCONY. IN DOING SO WE CREATE A SACRED PLACE – AN OASIS OF CALM WHERE WE CAN RECONNECT WITH OUR NATURAL STATE OF PEACEFULNESS AND TAKE REFUGE FROM THE DEMANDS OF DAILY LIFE. IN THIS CHAPTER WE LEARN HOW TO ALIGN OUR OUTDOOR SPACES WITH THE COSMOS. WE PAY TRIBUTE TO THE WEALTH AND VARIETY OF THE PLANT KINGDOM, DISCOVERING WHICH TREES AND FLOWERS PROVIDE TOOLS FOR BALANCING THE ELEMENTS AND THE *GUNAS*. USING THE VASTU PURUSHA MANDALA, WE LEARN HOW TO ORIENT OUR GARDEN SPACES TO ENHANCE THE FLOW OF *PRANA*, PAYING PARTICULAR ATTENTION TO THE USE OF WATER AND STONE. ULTIMATELY WE BRING NATURE INDOORS – CONNECTING OUR INNER AND OUTER WORLDS IN PERFECT HARMONY.

Vastu in the garden

No Vastu home is complete without an energized garden space. When replete with healthy plants, gardens possess a natural balance of the elements, and provide us with safe, protected places in which we can reconnect with the healing energies of nature. If you apply Vastu to the layout and design of your garden, you will be able to enhance these energies by maximizing the flow of *prana*.

When applying the Vastu Purusha Mandala (see pp.20–23) to a garden, consider the entire site (including the land on which the home stands) as a single unit. This will equip you with an overview of the site as a whole and the position of the house in relation to it. However, if your garden space forms an integral part of your home (as in a roof garden or balcony), you can apply the mandala to that space alone.

Keep the northeast quadrant of your garden relatively open, and install a water feature in the area to attract *prana*. Block the southwest corner to prevent the *prana* from escaping. The house itself is the ideal block, but if it is not located in the southwest of the plot then a screen of dense trees in a large garden, or a bushy, potted plant for a patio, conservatory or balcony, serves the same purpose.

We can balance the elements using shapes, sensory stimuli and the elements themselves: a rounded pond and contrasting textures of stones encourage Water and Air (above left); space stimulates Ether (above right); patterns of square paving stones promote Earth (below left); triangular topiary stimulates Fire (below right).

Other strong features, such as rock gardens, should also be placed in the southwest, where they are supported by Earth. Fire rules the southeast, providing the ideal conditions for bonfires and barbecues. Alternatively, this area is also suitable for a vegetable patch or orchard because Fire corresponds to the digestive system. For those with children, the northwest is the perfect place for a play area, where Air and Water favour movement and activity.

In general, try to adopt an uncluttered approach to your garden design. Dense foliage will obstruct the flow of energy, and a chaos of competing blooms will cause *prana* to eddy or stagnate.

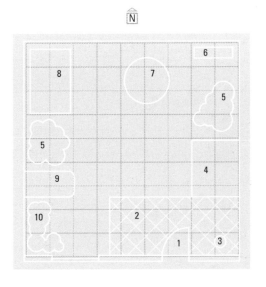

1	back door	6	bench
2	patio area	7	pond
3	barbecue	8	play area
4	vegetable patch	9	rock garden
5	flowerbed	10	bushes

Comfortable chairs arranged in a tranquil part of your garden or outdoor space will provide you with somewhere to rest and absorb the soothing energies of nature.

Borders and boundaries

In India images of ancestral heroes brandishing swords are placed at the edges of the village, facing outward to provide protection from external negative forces. The boundary of a township (or, for that matter, a property) has great significance in Vastu – it is the line that separates two opposing worlds (the inside from the outside, the natural from the humanmade, the sacred from the profane, the wild from the tame), and demands careful consideration.

Similarly, in the traditional practice of Vastu, builders erect the perimeter wall or fence of a property before they begin on the construction of the house itself. In this way new owners are safeguarded at the outset from the negative influences or inauspicious placements of the surrounding buildings and environment. For example, a pond (whether a neighbour's or a feature of the landscape) immediately to the southwest of your property would entice the *prana* out of your garden.

Of course, when most of us move into our homes we think more practically about the boundary fence or wall of our property. Does it grant seclusion? Does it shelter us from theft? Does it help to keep our children safe? These are all sensible questions that reflect the protective mood of Vastu.

Consider your boundary fence, hedge or wall. How high is it? The Vastu ideal is to

An opening in a wall (above) or holes in a wooden lattice fence (opposite) act as channels through which prana *can pass and are ideal for the northeastern boundaries of a property.*

have outer walls three-quarters the height of the front door, constructed from wood, stone or natural hedging. If you have iron railings surrounding your home, defuse their negative energy field by growing a flowering vine, such as clematis, over it.

The boundaries of your garden should allow *prana* to enter in the northeast, while containing it in the southwest. Lattice fences or walls with small openings will allow *prana* in. Thicker, more solid walls or fences are better in the southwest. If you have any hedging, the dense foliage of yew is ideal for southern and western aspects, while delicate beech hedges are better in the northeast. Alternatively, you can vary the heights of your fences to manipulate the pranic flow, keeping them lower in the northeast and higher in the southwest.

Gateways and pathways

Like thresholds and doorways inside the home, gateways to the garden perform a dual role in Vastu: they attract *prana* into the whole property, while also giving protection from negative external influences.

The main gateway of any home is the ceremonial opening to the property; it is also a primary avenue for incoming energy. Ideally, the gate itself should not exceed three-quarters the height of the front door. To create an effective barrier against negative forces, choose a gate built from materials that will not warp when subjected to the rigours of the environment. Seasoned wood gains solidity from its earthing properties and is ideal, although metals, such as wrought iron, offer an acceptable alternative. Bear in mind that your gateway gives the first impression of your home to visitors – decorative wooden carvings or delicate metalwork on your gate will present a welcoming aspect and attract *prana* into the property. Alternatively, you could grow flowering climbers over and around your gateway to achieve a similar result.

Hindus frequently place depictions of Ganesh (the elephant god revered as a remover of obstacles) on or near the main gate to preserve the home from evil influences. If there are *vedhas* near the gate,

above *Decorative metalwork and the natural beauty of a flowering climber attract* prana *through the gateway.* **opposite: left** *Swirling stone designs echo the meandering pattern of pranic flow.* **right** *The large, solid paving stones of this pathway connect strollers intimately to nature.*

such talismans are particularly useful. *Vedhas* are obstacles that restrict the flow of energy into a property. They can be anything from a nearby tree or telegraph pole to a road pointing directly toward the gate (known in Vastu as a *veedhi shola* or poison arrow). To counter these undesirable features, you can install your own talisman using a personal symbol of protection – perhaps a religious icon, a depiction of a lion, or even a simple light above the gate to ward off bad spirits at night.

In terms of positioning, Vastu practitioners believe that a garden gate located to the left of the front door (so that you walk to the right to reach the door) brings good luck into the home. More crucially, when you have the outer side of your garden gate facing in the same direction as

the outer side of your front door, there are fewer obstructions to the flow of energy between the two.

Driveways and pathways provide channels for *prana* – they direct the energy toward the home as well as distributing it throughout the garden. Any obstructions, such as overgrown bushes, potholes or precarious paving stones, will impede the flow of *prana*, so it is important to keep all pathways in your garden well-maintained.

You can further enhance the flow of energy by making your pathways form winding or crisscrossing patterns to echo the naturally meandering course of *prana*. If you have a long, straight path running across your garden, intercept the energy and encourage it to flow around large garden urns, ornaments or potted shrubs.

Build your pathways from natural materials, such as wood, stone or gravel. These will connect those walking in the garden more firmly to the earth and to nature in general.

The pathway that leads directly to your front door is particularly significant. In India many of the great shrines and temples are reached via a flight of steps. These remind supplicants of the difficult path toward the final liberation of the spirit. Steps leading up to your front door will prepare your visitors for entry into your home, imposing a symbolic rite of purification as they enter.

The patterned square of tiles serves to redirect the flow of prana *down the intercepting pathway.*

Trees and flowers

It is the trees, flowers and foliage that turn empty, outdoor spaces into living, breathing paradises. In Vastu all plants are believed to possess a natural balance of the five elements. Through this they encourage and regulate *prana*, creating energy fields that attract a variety of wildlife and quite literally bring the garden alive. To allow *prana* to flow through your garden, it is important to try to balance both the elements (see pp.28–31) and the *gunas* (see pp.32–3). This is even more the case when the layout of your garden does not accord with the Vastu ideal.

In India the ancient *rishis* planted groves of sacred trees called *panchavatis* to create powerful places for meditation. Each grove consisted of a central altar, surrounded by five indigenous trees: a fig tree in the east, a vilva in the north, a banyan in the west, an amalaki in the south, an asoka in the southeast. Create your own sacred grove by planting five saplings in a circle, or use potted dwarf trees for an immediate result. In either case, arrange the smaller trees in the north, east and southeast, and the taller trees in the south and west, to encourage and harness *prana*.

Fiery red flowers (below right) or, in more muted colour schemes, warm pink flowers (above left) stimulate rajas *and are ideal in the northwest or southeast of the garden. Flowers with pale and delicate petals (above right) are perfect for the northeast, where they promote* sattva, *while darker-coloured flowers with dense heads (below left) are best grown in the southwest, where they encourage* tamas.

You could base your choice of tree on the qualities that they symbolize. For example, fruit and flowering trees represent prosperity; evergreens symbolize longevity; and large trees with shady branches, such as the oak, connote wisdom.

According to Vastu, the placement of flowers in your garden can influence certain aspects of your life. Flowers in the north encourage prosperity; in the northwest, a happy social life; in the southwest, positive family and working lives; in the southeast, increased passion and romance; and in the east, fertility. If any of these aspects of life are troubling you, choose flowers that you find especially pleasing and plant them in the relevant place in your garden. By tending to them carefully, you will improve these areas of your life.

The patterns in which you organize your trees and flowers can be a means of balancing the elements in their appropriate quadrants. This may be necessary when the layout of your garden does not correspond to the Vastu ideal (see pp.122–5). For example, a barbecue should be located in the southeast (Fire) corner of the garden. However, if you have a fixed barbecue in the northwest, you risk weakening the Air and Water elements, which are resident in this area. You can strengthen these elements by incorporating crescents (the symbol of Air) and circles (the symbol of Water) into the patterns of your flowerbeds and bushes in the northwest.

This strategy can be applied to any section of the garden: focus on square shapes in the southwest to stimulate Earth;

triangular shapes in the southeast to promote Fire; diamond shapes in the northeast to encourage Ether.

In order to ensure that there is a balance of *gunas* in your garden, plant flowers and foliage that encourage the relevant *guna* in each quadrant. The *guna tamas* is a dense and inert energy that should predominate in the southwest of the garden. Plants with dark, dense leaves, such as the green laurel tree (*Prunus laurocerasus*) or the purple-brown perennial bronze bugle (*Ajuga reptans* 'Atropurpurea') possess a tamasic quality, and are therefore excellent choices for this area.

A tree such as the North American red maple (*Acer rubrum*) is ideal for the southeast or northwest corners of your garden where the warm, fiery colours of its blossoms, fruits and autumn leaves stimulate *rajas*. Red hot pokers (*Kniphofia uvaria*) are suitable flowers for these areas. They have bright-red, tubular heads with strap-shaped, dark green leaves. In a more muted colour scheme, the lilac-to-pink flowers of wild bergamot (*Monarda fistulosa*) have a similar, if less powerful, effect when they blossom in the summer.

In the northeast of your garden, where an abundance of *sattva* encourages *prana* to enter, choose delicately leaved trees and flowers in cool, pale shades. The shimmering silver-green leaves of the white willow (*Salix alba* var. *sericea*) and the fragile white blossoms of jasmine (*Jasminum*) are perfect for this purpose.

Try to plan your garden so that there is a harmonious balance of shapes and

colours throughout the year. It can be helpful to draw up a chart or calendar on which to block out the flowering periods for the different varieties of trees and plants, bearing in mind that some species are annuals, to be replanted every twelve months, whereas others are perennials, reappearing in the same spot each year. Intersperse flowers with shrubs or foliage. This helps to prevent periods in which certain areas of the garden are lacking in life and energy.

The general style of your garden should complement that of your home. For example, a formal and structured garden based on a geometric design, laid out with clipped topiary and carefully patterned flowerbeds, would enhance the classical lines of either a period home or modern ground-floor apartment. A looser, more casual approach, which focuses on fluid forms with rambling vines and a seemingly haphazard profusion of trees and flowers, would dovetail with the rustic charm of a country cottage or rural retreat.

Whatever type of garden you have, it is important to root out diseased plants. In Vastu such plants are believed to suffer from an energy imbalance that can disrupt the harmony of the garden. Likewise, steer clear of spiky or thorny trees, such as pine or holly. These repel *prana* and may sap the energies of your garden.

These trees are most appropriate in the northwest and southeast of a garden, where their fiery autumnal colours stimulate rajas. *The variety of tree heights encourages* prana *to flow more freely.*

Fountains and ponds

An abundance of water is essential to the life of any garden. Water ensures that there is pure, ionized air, fertile soil and a proliferation of wildlife. In Vastu water attracts *prana* naturally, and stimulates its flow throughout the property as a whole.

You can introduce a water feature into your garden whatever its size. If you have a very small outdoor space (perhaps a roof terrace or balcony), you could simply arrange some pebbles in a ceramic dish and fill it with water. In a larger property you have scope to be more ambitious – you could install a pond with an elegant fountain or direct a stream of running water over a cascade of rocks.

According to Vastu, the running water of fountains and streams has particularly energizing effects on the property. Like paths, streams carry energy around the garden and should, ideally, follow a rambling course, like *prana*. The melodic gurgle of flowing water not only soothes the mind, but also promotes Ether (stimulated by hearing), which predominates in the northeast. This is the subtlest element and is responsible for initiating pranic flow into a space. Light refracting through fountain spray produces rainbows, which highlight the energizing effects of the sun.

Circles or other curved shapes are most appropriate for ponds because the

In Vastu it is believed that what is reflected in the water is as important as the feature itself. Rounded forms, such as these stone sculptures, produce ideal reflections because the circle is the symbol of Water.

circle is the symbol for Water. Do not imagine that you need a grand garden to have a pond – a bricked and lined corner of even a small garden can be enough. Many garden centres stock ingenious pond kits suitable for gardens of all sizes, or you could create your own free-standing pond from a barrel cut in half.

If there is no fountain in your pond, introduce water weeds and goldfish to keep the water free from stagnation. You could also cultivate waterlilies (symbolizing the abundance of the world) on the surface of the pond, and introduce reeds and interesting rocks around the edges to create a sense of harmony between the pond and the surrounding natural environment.

Because water attracts *prana* the most suitable location for water features is the northeast quadrant where *prana* enters the garden. Try to set the feature toward either the north or the east of the quadrant. The north is the realm of Kubera, god of wealth and healing. Increasing the flow of *prana* to this area will reward you with greater prosperity and improved health. The east is governed by Indra, the Vedic god of renewal. Increasing the flow of energy to this region will enhance your fertility, wisdom and spiritual growth.

left *Growing waterlilies on the surface of your pond will attract abundance and wealth into your life.*
right *The swirling patterns of contrasting coloured stones beneath the water create interesting visual effects and mimic the movement of* prana.

# Rock gardens

Mountains have always evoked profound responses in humankind. Their height, strength and sheer majesty have given rise to powerful symbolism in traditions all over the world. According to Hindu myth, Mount Meru, the abode of the gods, is believed to be the centre of the cosmos, and forms the Earth's spiritual axis. In Vastu it is believed that rock gardens echo such sacred landscapes, bringing the grounded spirit of mountains into the domestic garden to provide a firm bedrock of support for the entire property.

The size of your rock garden should be proportionate to your garden as a whole. This ensures that Earth (represented by the rocks) does not outweigh the other elements. In a small space you can construct a miniature rock garden in a container. In larger gardens build rough stone walls to form a series of terraced beds, or mound up a small corner of your garden with soil and embed a variety of rocks into the earth.

The ideal location for a rock garden is the southwest where Earth provides support for the heavy weight of the rocks. In this area rocks help us to tap the knowledge and strength of our ancestors – on a sunny day try using your rock garden as a focus for meditation on ancestral wisdom.

The apparently random arrangement of these large rocks create a natural effect. The fiery yellows and pinks of the flowers and the warm brown of the rocks stimulate rajas *and would be especially appropriate for a rock garden in the northwest.*

Rock features positioned elsewhere in your garden can cause blockages in the pranic flow. However, if you already have an established rock garden you can remedy an inauspicious placement with strategic choices of colours for your rocks and plants. Select colours that will stimulate the *guna* appropriate to the area in which the rock garden is located. For example, in a northwest or southeast rock garden you could combine warm-coloured sandstone with the fiery, crimson flowers of Henderson's shooting star (*Dodecatheon hendersonii*) to promote *rajas*. In a northeast rock garden you could pair pale, grey limestone with the pure, white flowers and beautiful, silver-encrusted leaves of *Saxifraga* 'Tumbling Waters' (Saxifragaceae) to enhance *sattva*.

Places of rest

Many Indian gardens have summerhouses (some of very simple structure) where the residents can enjoy the scents, colours, textures and sounds of the garden; they are places of rest where the spirit can be nourished by the healing energies of nature.

If you do not have space for a summerhouse, place a simple bench in a shady area from which you can enjoy the delights of your garden. The open northeast corner is the ideal location for this "zone of tranquillity". Here you will enjoy the energizing benefits of incoming *prana*.

When buying or building a summerhouse, choose natural materials, such as wood or stone, because these reinforce our

above *The trellis work adorning this summerhouse allows* prana *to flow through the structure.* **opposite** *A bench tucked away in a corner provides a secluded spot from which to appreciate your garden.*

deep connection with the environment. Seasoned wood is perfect because it can withstand all weathers.

The shape and design of a summerhouse dictates its optimum location within the garden. Square, solid structures represent Earth and are best positioned in the southwest where they help to prevent *prana* from escaping – elsewhere they tend to restrict the flow of *prana*.

Octagonal or round structures assist the flow of energy and are ideal for northwest or southeast locations where *prana* is in full flux. (Round summerhouses are particularly suitable for the northwest where Water, symbolized by a circle, is dominant.) You can position them on the lawn, provided they do not obstruct the vulnerable points of Vastu Purusha in the centre.

🪷 Nature indoors

The main aim of Vastu is to establish harmony between ourselves, our homes and the surrounding natural world. A simple way to achieve this connection (especially if you live in an apartment with no outdoor space) is to bring nature indoors, incorporating plants, flowers and other natural elements, such as fruits and vegetables, into the design of your home.

As we have seen, the multisensory appeal of natural forms means that we can use them to balance the elements (see pp.28–31), while their striking colours offer us great scope to correct the distribution of the *gunas* (see pp.32–3). Most plants and flowers attract positive energy, so we can use them more generally to regulate the flow of *prana* through a space.

Prana enters a room or home from the northeast. Placing flowers in this region will energize and enhance all aspects of your life. More specifically, as in a garden, you can position plants and flowers in other parts of a space to boost particular aspects of your life (see p.134). However, it is important to remember that large plants will block rather than promote pranic flow when placed in the northeast; instead, they should be positioned in the southwest where they will be supported by Earth.

As with the general decoration of your home, to promote fully the free flow

Potted grasses provide an alternative to flowers in the dining room. Their delicate forms are suggestive of curling flames of Fire – the element associated with the body's digestive system.

of *prana* adopt a minimal approach, with a few choice plants or flower arrangements positioned strategically. Swamping your home with foliage is counterproductive because it will darken your rooms, limiting rather than enhancing pranic flow. (In particular, avoid filling your bedroom with plants because at night they release carbon dioxide.) However, if you have a conservatory, feel free to fill it with plants – *prana* flows easily through conservatories, even when they are filled with dense foliage, because they are made of glass and are therefore suffused with natural light.

Certain plants repel *prana* and are unsuitable for the home. As a general rule avoid all plants with thorns or very spiky leaves, such as cacti and thistles – particularly in the northeast quadrant where they

prevent wealth from entering the home. For the same reason remove the thorns from any roses that you bring into the house. Flowers or plants that are wilting or sick also deter *prana*, so it is very important to remove dead leaves and flower heads as well as replacing any dried flowers or pot-pourri when they become faded and dusty.

Bear in mind that displaying certain flowers can enhance the atmosphere of a room. For example, in the hallway bold gerberas in sunny yellows and cheeky pinks offer a cheerful welcome for visitors to the home; in the dining room the velvety blooms of scarlet roses form a seductive centrepiece for romantic dinners; and in the bedroom the delicate buds of grape hyacinth and lily of the valley provide a restful focus before sleep.

When selecting flowers consider the general style of your home. The baroque grandeur of roses will echo the ornate mouldings of a period home, while the elegant simplicity of a single arum lily or heliconia will complement the structural geometrics of a modern apartment.

Of course, in Vastu the main reason for incorporating plantlife into our homes is to reconnect with the natural world. Synchronizing our homes with the cyclical rhythm of the changing seasons reminds us of the ebb and flow of life and death. We can honour each season with a suitable display of flowers, foliage or other natural elements. In spring, flower bulbs, such as hyacinths, remind us of the rebirth of nature, while yellow daffodils or tulips bring the hope of sunnier days to come. In summer we can echo the exuberant spirit of the season with flamboyant sunflowers, extravagant blue peonies and blousy pink roses. Later in the year chocolate cosmos and orange gladioli bring the rusty colours of fall into the home and rich displays of vegetables, such as pumpkin, gourd and dried corn, pay tribute to the harvest. During the barren months of winter, evergreens, such as juniper and mistletoe, remind us of the eternal spirit, and glorious amaryllis flowers in seasonal red or white brighten the dark days.

An imposing display of brilliant yellow spring flowers irradiates the room. Although placed in the window, the fragile sprays enhance rather than block the flow of incoming light.

Conclusion: Vastu now

For centuries the dominant models of Western thought have centred on a dualistic perception of the world, in which we, as human beings, are defined as separate from (and superior to) our environment. This artificial separation between human and world has permitted the exploitation of our surroundings in the name of technological advancement – to the detriment of many of the world's natural ecosystems.

It is only in recent years that the human as well as environmental costs of these damaging activities has become clear. In polluting the world we pollute our bodies, for we are dependent upon the resources of the world, such as food, water and air, for our survival.

It is an understanding of this interdependence between ourselves and our environment that forms the basis of Vastu, which seeks to align living spaces with their inhabitants and the cosmos. In doing so Vastu works to heal the rift between human beings and their surroundings – a split never wider than today. For this reason Vastu has perhaps greater relevance in the modern world than ever before.

In practising Vastu we learn, and show, respect for the natural world, as well as ourselves. By encouraging such an attitude of responsibility, Vastu empowers us to effect positive changes in the immediate environments of our homes and gardens, to improve the lives of both ourselves and those around us.

Many of the changes recommended by Vastu work to reinforce our connection with the natural world. As we have seen, these include building our homes from natural, nontoxic materials that protect the inhabitants, and orienting our homes according to the movement of the sun – thereby filling them with an abundance of natural light. On a more subtle energetic level, Vastu helps us to manipulate the energies of the home (the five elements and three *gunas*) to reflect the balance within our bodies and the cosmos.

As a spiritual science Vastu also extends beyond these primarily physical concerns to touch on the deeper emotional and psychological aspects of our relationship with our surroundings. As the Vedic scriptures remind us, our identity – our sense of who and what we are – is forged through an intimate relationship with our surroundings, mediated via the five senses, our doorways to the external world. It is for this reason that Vastu places such emphasis on the creation of living spaces with moods and atmospheres uniquely adapted to suit our individual needs and desires.

Whether you are redesigning your home from scratch, or focusing on a single room, the basic Vastu principles remain the same. Remember that even small improvements can make a difference. An extra lamp to illuminate a corner, a bright rajasic cushion on a chair, a clear space in the centre of a room – all are simple touches that can have a profound impact on the flow of energy or *prana* through your home. These changes represent the first tentative steps toward a healthier and happier lifestyle, a small but significant contribution to making the world a better place.

Further reading

BABU, B. N. *Handbook of Vastu*, UBS Publishers' Distributors Ltd (New Delhi, India), 1997.

BAHOLYODHIN, O. *Living with Zen*, Charles E. Tuttle Co. (Boston, US) and Duncan Baird Publishers (London), 2000.

CHAKRABARTI, V. *Indian Architectural Theory*, Curzon Press (New York and London), 1998.

COX, K. *Vastu Living*, Marlowe & Company (New York), 2000.

CRAZE, R. *Vaastu*, Carlton Books (London), 2001.

FEUERSTEIN, G. *The Shambhala Encyclopedia of Yoga*, Shambala Publications (Boston and London), 1997.

ISHERWOOD, C. *Ramakrishna and his Disciples*, Simon & Schuster (New York), 1959 and Shepheard-Walwyn (London),1986.

LAGATREE, K. M. *Feng Shui*, Villard Books (New York), 1996.

MAGEE, V. *Archetype Design*, Archetype Design Publications (Taos, New Mexico), 1999.

MASTER LAM KAM CHUEN *The Feng Shui Handbook*, Henry Holt (New York), 1996 and Gaia Books (London), 1995.

PANDEY, P.B. *Sacred Plants of India*, Shree Publishing House (New Delhi, India),1989.

PEGRUM, J. *Vastu Vidya*, Three Rivers Press (Three Rivers, Michigan) and Gaia Books (London), 2000.

RADHAKRISHNAN & MOORE *Sourcebook in Indian Philosophy*, Princeton University Press (Princeton, New Jersey), 1957.

RAO, D. M. *Vastu Shilpa Shaastra*, Galgotia Publications Ltd (New Delhi, India), 1997.

TOO, L. *Lillian Too's Chinese Wisdom*, Friedman/Fairfax Publishing (New York) and CICO Books (London), 2001.

WALLER, M. & BRADBURY, D. *Fusion Interiors*, Watson-Guptill Publications (New York) and Pavilion Books (London), 2000.

WALTER, D. & CHISLETT, H. *Organized Living*, The Lyons Press (Guildford, US) and Conran Octopus (London), 2001.

WARRIER, G. & GUNAWANT D. *The Complete Illustrated Guide to Ayurveda*, Element Books (Shaftesbury, Dorset), 1997.

WATERSTONE, R. *India: The Cultural Companion*, Thorsons (New York) and Duncan Baird Publishers (London), 2002.

For information on the work and designs of Juliet Pegrum, readers may visit her website at the following location: www.vastuvidya.com, or email her on julietpegrum@vastuvidya.com.

Index

triangle, as symbol 31
triangular sites 43, 44

V

valuables 101
Varuna 21, 22
Vastu (Vastu Vidya) 8–9, 16, 146, 150–51
    applying *see* gardens *and individual rooms*
    and Ayurveda 14, 34
    Feng Shui and 14
    and individuals 11, 23, 151
    meaning of name 14
    and mythology 18–23, 24
    origins and history 14–15
    and *prana* 34–7, 58
    theoretical basis 34–5, 43, 142, 151
    and Western homes 15–16, 46
    and yoga 14, 34
    see also rishis
Vastu Purusha *see* Purusha
Vastu Purusha Mandala 20–24, 40, 122
Vasus 21–3
Vayu 22, 23
Vedas, the 14–15, 16, 34, 46, 151
vedhas 45, 128–30
Vedic architecture 15, 16
Vedic civilization 23
Vedic disciplines 34
    see also Ayurveda; Vastu; yoga

vegetables 31, 125
ventilation 79, 94, 114
    see also windows
verandas 49
vibrations 26, 28
    see also energy
Vishwakarma 15

W

walls 20, 126–7
Water (element) 28–9, 87, 90, 93, 95, 108
    circular sites and 44
    and eating 83–4
    and hallways 65
    and kitchens 75, 76, 79
    and living rooms 66–8, 72
    and *prana* 141
    and purification 90
    and *rajas* 32
    symbolic representations, and
        strengthening/appeasing 29, 31, 71, 72,
        104, 138
    and the Vastu Purusha Mandala 21, 22
    and workplaces 118
water features 29, 31, 122, 138–41
wealth 72, 79, 94, 101, 141, 148
white 52
windows 29, 36, 46–8, 49, 62, 97
    sitting by 88, 94

see also ventilation
wisdom 141, 142
wood 48, 49, 62, 66, 76, 127, 145
    for furniture 76, 80, 84, 88, 101, 117
    for gates and paths 128, 131
work 86, 87, 88–9, 118
workplaces 116–19
    see also studies

Y

Yajurveda 14–15
Yama 21, 22, 117
yantras 45
yoga 14, 26, 34, 72, 110, 113

Z

zones of tranquillity 41, 72, 89

Acknowledgments

The publisher would like to thank the following people, museums and photographic libraries for permission to reproduce their material. Every care has been taken to trace copyright holders. However, if we have omitted anyone we apologise and will, if informed, make corrections in any future edition.

t = top   b = bottom
c = centre   l = left
r = right

Page 1tl Ken Hayden/Red Cover, London; 1tr Ken Hayden/Red Cover; 1bl Inside Stock Image/Interior Archive, London; 1br Andrew Wood/Interior Archive; 5 Ray Main/Mainstream, Hertfordshire; 6t Ray Main/Mainstream; 6b Andrew Wood /DBP; 7t Andrew Wood/Interior Archive; 7b W. Broadhurst /A-Z Botanical, London; 12 Ken Hayden/Red Cover; 16–17 D. Beatty/Robert Harding Picture Library, London; 16 inset India Office Library/Bridgeman Art Library, London; 19 Robert Harding Picture Library; 25 Sue Carpenter/Axiom, London; 27 Simon Upton /Interior Archive; 30tl Fritz von Schulenberg /Interior Archive; 30tr Simon Upton /Interior Archive; 30bl Ray Main/Mainstream; 30br Andrew Wood/Interior Archive; 33 Elizabeth Whiting Associates, London; 35 Ianthe Ruthven/Interior Archive; 37 Chris Caldicott/Axiom; 38 Ken Hayden/Red Cover; 42 Ray Main/Mainstream/ Architect Patrick Gwynne; 47 James Mitchell/Red Cover; 51t James Mitchell/Red Cover; 51b Elizabeth Whiting; 55l Gaelle Boulicault, Australia; 55r Ray Main/Mainstream/ Designer Vincente Wolfe; 56l Andrew Twort/Red Cover; 56c Gaelle Boulicault; 56r Ray Main/Mainstream/ Designer Vincente Wolfe; 59 Ray Main/Mainstream ; 60 Inside Stock Image/Interior Archive; 63 Andrew Wood/Interior Archive; 64 Fritz von Schulenberg/ Interior Archive; 67 Andrew Wood/Interior Archive; 69l Ray Main/Mainstream; 69r James Morris/ Axiom; 70tl Andrew Wood/Interior Archive; 70tr Ray Main/ Mainstream; 70bl James Merrell/Red Cover; 70br Andrew Wood/Interior Archive; 72–73 Andreas von Einsiedel/Red Cover; 74 Ken Hayden/ Red Cover; 77 James Morris /Axiom; 78l Richard Powers/Redback/Arcaid, London; 78r Ray Main/ Mainstream; 80 Ray Main /Mainstream ; 82tl David Hiscock/DBP; 82tr Ray Main/Mainstream; 82bl Ray Main/Mainstream; 82br Christopher Drake/Red Cover; 84 Simon Upton/Interior Archive; 85 Simon Upton/Interior Archive; 86 Peter Cook/ VIEW, London; 89 Verity Welstead/Red Cover; 91 John Kerr/VIEW; 92l Andrew Wood /Interior Archive; 92r Andrew Wood/DBP; 96 Andrew Wood/Interior Archive; 99 Gaelle Boulicault; 100t Dennis Gilbert/VIEW; 100b Ray Main/Mainstream; 103tl Ray Main/Mainstream; 103tr Ray Main/ Mainstream; 103bl Ken Hayden/Red Cover; 103br David Hiscock/DBP; 104 Tim Beddow/Interior Archive; 105 Graham Atkins-Hughes/Red Cover; 106 Tim Beddow/Interior Archive; 109 Fritz von Schulenberg/Interior Archive; 111 Andreas von Einsiedel/Red Cover; 113 Elizabeth Whiting; 114tl Churchill/Arcaid; 114tr Peter Cook/VIEW; 114bl Verity Welstead/Red Cover; 114br Andreas von Einsiedel/Red Cover; 120 Andrew Wood/Interior Archive; 123tl Adrian Thomas/A-Z Botanical; 123tr Hugh Palmer/Red Cover; 123bl Elizabeth Whiting; 123br James Guilam/A-Z Botanical; 124l Tim Beddow/Interior Archive; 124r Ken Hayden/ Red Cover; 126 John Glover/ The Garden Picture Library, London; 127 Ken Hayden/Red Cover; 128 Jerry Pavia/The Garden Picture Library, London; 129l Charlotte Mellis/Edifice; 129r Anthony Cooper/A-Z Botanical; 130 Sarah Jackson/Edifice; 132tl Andrew Lawson, Oxford; 132tr Andrew Lawson; 132bl Andrew Lawson; 132br Andrew Lawson; 137 W. Broadhurst/A-Z Botanical; 139 Ken Hayden/Red Cover; 140l W. Broadhurst/A-Z Botanical; 140r Juliet Greene/The Garden Picture Library; 143 David England/The Garden Picture Library; 144 Philippa Lewis/Edifice 145 Andrew Lawson; 146-7 Peter Cook/VIEW; 148 Fritz von Schulenberg/Interior Archive

Author's acknowledgments
I would like to thank Brenda Pegrum for proof-reading and editing the initial text, and my editor, Lucy Latchmore, and the team at DBP for crafting this material into a lovely book.

Understanding
Telephone
Electronics

Third Edition

Third Edition
  Revised by: Stephen J. Bigelow
  Process Control Engineer
  Bedford, MA

First and
Second
Editions by: John L. Fike, Ph.D., P.E.
  Adj. Assoc. Professor of Electrical Engineering
  Southern Methodist University

  George E. Friend
  Consultant, Telecommunications
  Dallas, TX

Newnes

Boston   Oxford   Johannesburg
Melbourne   New Delhi   Singapore

Copyright © 1997 by Butterworth-Heinemann

This book was originally developed by:
The Staff of Texas Instruments Information Publishing Center
Copyright © 1983 and 1984 by Texas Instruments, Inc.
Copyright © 1991 by SAMS, a division of Macmillan Computer Publishing

Newnes is an imprint of Butterworth-Heinemann

ᴿ A member of the Reed Elsevier group

∞ Recognizing the importance of what has been written, Butterworth-Heinemann
prints its books on acid-free paper whenever possible.

ISBN 0-7506-9944-2

Printed in the United States of America
10 9 8 7 6